PREFACE

Welcome to "God Does Wonders: A 30 Day Prayer Devotional with Powerful Testimonies."

In a world filled with uncertainty and challenges, where our faith is constantly put to the test, prayer remains our unshakable anchor and the bridge to a deeper, more intimate relationship with our Creator. This book takes us on a journey that explores the power of prayer and ignites a passion for a life aligned with the remarkable acts of God.

The book's title, "God Does Wonders," captures the heart of the Christian journey. It symbolizes the incredible and life-altering moments when we sincerely seek God through prayer. Roland Bahozi has expertly created a guide for a deep dive into prayer—a 30-day journey that renews our spirits, strengthens our faith, and opens us to the miraculous.

This book draws inspiration from the Book of Acts, which tells the remarkable story of the early church's powerful transformation through prayer. Like the apostles, we, too, can experience God's extraordinary work. Roland encourages us to adopt the "ACTS Lifestyle" as our spiritual guide—a simple acronym for Adoration, Confession, Thanksgiving, and Supplication. Through scripture and personal stories, these four pillars of prayer help us navigate life's challenges with grace, faith, and a connection to God.

As you start this 30-day prayer journey, may it touch your heart, strengthen your faith, and enhance your bond with God. May you feel God's presence and see His amazing responses to your prayers. "God Does Wonders" isn't just a book; it's an opportunity to meet God in your everyday life.

Open these pages with anticipation. Get ready to be motivated and uplifted. Let your spirit be awakened to the extraordinary. Join us on this sacred journey where prayer transforms from a habit into a way of life, a wellspring of strength, and a testament to the incredible deeds of our faithful God.

In His grace and love

GOD DOES WONDERS

A 30 Day Prayer Devotional with Powerful Testimonies

By Roland Bahozi

PUBLIC TRANSFORMATION
THE NETHERLANDS

GOD DOES WONDERS
by Roland Bahozi

Published by
PUBLIC TRANSFORMATION,
Moerkapelle, The Netherlands

Copyright © 2023 ROLAND BAHOZI

ISBN: 9789493274105
NUR: 707

Public Transformation – For Books with Impact!

TABLE OF CONTENTS

INTRODUCTION

Prayer is a universal language, a divine connection that transcends boundaries and unites us as human beings. In every corner of the world, individuals from diverse walks of life find comfort, hope, and strength in the power of prayer. Whether you've felt the compelling call to intercede on behalf of another or you stand in need of intercession yourself, the act of prayer is a profound and deeply personal experience. We all have friends, family members, or colleagues who could benefit from the uplifting embrace of prayer, making intercession an essential and heartfelt journey that we embark upon together.

1 Timothy 2:1: *"First of all, then, I urge that petitions (specific requests), prayers, intercessions (prayers for others) and thanksgivings be offered on behalf of all people"*.

If you've been experiencing the desire to pray for someone, or perhaps for yourself, and you're unsure about where to begin, you've taken a significant step in the right direction by choosing this devotional book. It's essential to understand that the most important question isn't "how to pray," but "why we pray?"

Points to Consider

- True prayer is born out of genuine love for others.
- When you pray, you align with God's heart, as seen in Ezekiel 22:30: "I looked for someone among them who would build up the wall and stand before me in the gap on behalf of the land so I would not have to destroy it, but I found no one."
- Prayer can reach places that our feet cannot. It is a divine bridge that carries our petitions to the throne of grace.
- Prayer stands as the most potent weapon against strongholds, regardless of their nature. It's the tool we use to dismantle the fortresses that hinder progress, healing, and transformation.
- To overcome temptation, turn to prayer. In those moments of weakness, when the snares of the world tighten their grip, prayer becomes our lifeline, strengthening our resolve to resist.
- Prayer is the key that can unlock even the most tightly sealed doors. When obstacles seem insurmountable, when paths are obstructed, prayer can swing open the doors of opportunity and usher in new possibilities.
- Through prayer, you can establish a profound connection with God through the Holy Spirit. It's not merely words spoken into the void; it's a direct line to the divine, a channel through which the Spirit imparts wisdom, guidance, and comfort.
- Faith comes to life and is actively engaged through prayer. As we lift our hearts and voices in prayer, faith is ignited, moving mountains, and achieving the extraordinary.

One day at a time Devotional

In this prayer and intercession devotional, I invite you to join me on a 30-day journey of intercession, as we lift up various groups of people in prayer. Within each chapter, you will also find my personal experiences and testimonies of encounters with God. These testimonies serve as a testament to the incredible power of God, and it is my hope that they will inspire and ignite a deeper connection with the Father within you. At the end of each chapter, you will discover a 'Personal Prayer Guide.' This invaluable section provides you with the opportunity to jot down the names of individuals you are interceding for, along with your own personal prayer points and requests.

As you read this book, you'll witness the remarkable ways in which prayer and the guidance of the Holy Spirit have brought about transformative experiences in my life. I believe that, just as I have encountered His amazing grace, you too can experience the profound blessings that come through prayer.

May the Lord richly bless you and shower His grace upon you throughout these 30 days of intercession and devotion."

CHAPTER 1

PRAYER AS INTERCESSION

Let me share a remarkable story that unfolded about a year and a half ago. A single mother had a heartfelt desire for her daughter to study abroad. Together, they took the courageous step of applying to a university, eagerly anticipating a response for a long, trying year and a half, but none arrived.

Feeling distraught by the prolonged silence, the single mother reached out to me for support. Recognizing the power of prayer, I suggested that we embark on a journey of faith and intercession. With her consent, we decided to involve her daughter in this spiritual endeavor.

Our prayers were anything but generic; they were infused with specificity and faith. We fervently implored the Lord to unlock any hidden barriers, to pave the way for their dream to come true. It was during this time of prayer that a profound conviction settled in our hearts—a message from the Lord: "You will receive an email from the university."

With hope and anticipation in our hearts, we continued to pray.

The very next morning, as the sun began to rise, I was greeted by a message that had arrived the previous day at 4:00 PM. It was a momentous email—an acceptance letter from the university!

Dear friends, this story serves as a powerful reminder of the incredible potency of prayer. It illustrates that indeed, prayer is the key to unlocking doors, transforming circumstances, and making the impossible possible. Through faith-filled prayers, we witnessed the hand of the divine intervening in their lives, bringing forth an acceptance they had longed for.

In moments of uncertainty and delay, remember that prayer is not merely a formality; it is a profound connection with the Almighty—a channel through which blessings, breakthroughs, and miracles flow.

Brethren, do you see that prayer is all we need? This is why:

1. **The Wisdom in Prayer:** Prayer is not merely a conversation; it's a divine exchange where we acquire wisdom from the source of all knowledge.
2. **Casting Your Cares:** When the weight of burdens, worries, and cares becomes too heavy to bear, remember that there is relief in taking them to the Lord in prayer.
3. **Transformation Through Prayer:** Unfavorable circumstances can find their course altered through the transformative power of prayer.
4. **Hearts Changed Through Prayer:** Just as circumstances can change, so can your own heart and the hearts of people. Prayer has the capacity to touch and transform the most stubborn of hearts.

5. **Prayer for Justice:** To combat injustice and address the presence of evil, it is vital to act, but equally, if not more important, is the act of earnest prayer.
6. **The Power of Love in Prayer:** Our responsibility is not to change others; it is to love them through prayer. The ultimate responsibility for change rests in God's hands.
7. **Uplifting Spirits:** In times of despair and discouragement, prayer has the remarkable ability to uplift our spirits, bringing hope and renewal.
8. **Walking in Jesus's Footsteps:** When we engage in prayer, we are walking in the footsteps of Jesus, aligning our hearts and actions with His divine will.

John 17:20: *"I do not pray for these alone [it is not for their sake only that I make this request], but also for [all] those who [will ever] believe and trust in Me through their message."*

Prayer Reaches Anyone / Anywhere You want

Some things are beyond our physical, emotional, and economic strength because as we look at them, we tell ourselves that we cannot do anything about them.

No, there is something you can do – pray.

In fact, the Bible recommends us to pray without ceasing.

Joel 1:13 says, *"Clothe yourselves with sackcloth and lament (cry out in grief), O priests; Wail, O ministers of the altar! Come, spend the night in sackcloth [and pray without ceasing], O ministers of my God, For the grain offering and the drink offering are withheld from the house of your God."*

And 1 Thessalonians 5:17 adds, *"Be unceasing and persistent in prayer."*

But what is prayer?

Prayer transcends the mere exchange of ideas or persuading the other side of the desk. It is a sacred communion, a fellowship with a personal God who eagerly anticipates your voice.

It is the humble act of baring your soul before a God who listens to your every plea. It represents the recognition of our human frailty and limitations in the presence of an all-powerful, boundless Creator. These attitudes are underpinned by a profound conviction and unwavering acknowledgment of the existence of God. It is, in essence, a profound communion and fellowship with a personal God who not only listens but eagerly desires to hear your voice.

"Call to me and I will answer you, and will tell you great and hidden things that you have not known." — Jeremiah 33:3 (ESV)

In prayer, we engage in the intimate act of unveiling our hearts before the Divine, a God who not only hears but responds to our cries. It is the unreserved pouring out of our hopes, fears, and aspirations, confident in the knowledge that our Heavenly Father is attentive to our every word.

> *"The righteous cry out, and the Lord hears them; He delivers them from all their troubles."*
> — Psalm 34:17 (NIV)

Yet, prayer also serves as a solemn acknowledgment of our inherent human limitations. We stand humbly before an infinite and all-powerful God, recognizing our inadequacies in the grandeur of His presence.

"Humble yourselves, therefore, under the mighty hand of God so that at the proper time He may exalt you, casting all your anxieties on Him, because He cares for you."
— 1 Peter 5:6-7 (ESV)

This act of prayer is anchored in an unwavering conviction of God's existence and His willingness to engage with His creation. It is not a one-sided conversation but a divine dialogue where the Creator of the universe actively seeks communion with His beloved children.

"Ask, and it will be given to you; seek, and you will find; knock, and it will be opened to you."
— Matthew 7:7 (ESV)

In prayer, we draw near to the One who sustains all things, offering our gratitude, petitions, and confessions, knowing that our relationship with Him transcends earthly bounds. It is a sacred privilege to converse with the Almighty, to find comfort in His presence, and to experience His transformative power in our lives. Prayer is the divine connection between our finite existence and the infinite love of God.

Hebrews 11:6: *"But without faith it is impossible to [walk with God and] please Him, for whoever comes [near] to God must [necessarily] believe that God exists and that He rewards those who [earnestly and diligently] seek Him."*

Pray with Expectation: Reaping God's Rewards

Approach your prayers with great anticipation, for our faithful God indeed rewards those who earnestly seek Him through prayer.

> *"Ask and it will be given to you; seek and you will find; knock and the door will be opened to you."*
> — Matthew 7:7 (NIV)

Within the pages of this book, you'll discover a collection of my heartfelt prayers and profound encounters with God. These reflections can serve as a wellspring of inspiration for your own prayer life, guiding you on how to approach your conversations with the Almighty.

> *"The prayer of a righteous person is powerful and effective."* — James 5:16b (NIV)

But this book isn't just a passive read; it's an invitation to actively engage with the divine. You'll encounter blank pages within its depths, awaiting the ink of your own prayers, hopes, and impressions. Feel free to use these pages as a canvas for your personal petitions, a place to pour out your heart, and an altar for your deepest desires.

> *"Pour out your heart like water before the face of the Lord. Lift your hands toward Him for the life of your young children."* — Lamentations 2:19a (NKJV)

Additionally, you can utilize these pages to inscribe the names of individuals who occupy your thoughts and prayers. Keep a record of those for whom you intercede, so you may faithfully lift them up before the Creator.

"I urge, then, first of all, that petitions, prayers, intercession and thanksgiving be made for all people." 1 Timothy 2:1 (NIV)

Moreover, this space is reserved for you to document the remarkable testimonies and divine interventions that transpire through the power of prayer. Celebrate the answered prayers, miracles, and transformations that bear witness to God's profound work in your life and the lives of others.

"I will give thanks to you, Lord, with all my heart; I will tell of all your wonderful deeds." — Psalm 9:1 (NIV)

So, as you embark on this prayerful journey, may you find inspiration, guidance, and a tangible record of God's faithfulness. Use this book not only to learn how to pray but also to leave an indelible imprint of your communion with the Creator.

PRAYER FOR LEADERS

"Pray for kings and all who are in [positions of] high authority, so that we may live a peaceful and quiet life in all godliness and dignity." (1 Timothy 2:2)

Heavenly Father,

We heed your call to pray for our leaders and express our gratitude for every individual you have chosen to rise to positions of leadership.

We beseech you, Lord, to grant them a servant's heart, instilling in them a deep desire to serve their communities with humility and compassion.

May they be vessels through which your divine presence shines, allowing their people to see your grace, love, and wisdom reflected in their leadership.

Father, we pray that you keep their hearts securely in your hands, filling them with your boundless love and guiding them in all they do. May they experience the genuine love and respect of those they lead, becoming instruments of unity and goodwill in Jesus' name.

In your divine presence, we offer these prayers, trusting in your wisdom and grace. Amen.

PRAYER FOR SECULAR LEADERS

Dear Lord,

We come before you with gratitude in our hearts for the leaders of all 195 nations across the globe. We express our appreciation for the dedicated business leaders who guide our world's economies and the tireless efforts of police commanders, military leaders, and all those who serve as secular authorities. Today, we lift up our heartfelt prayers on their behalf.

We beseech you, Lord, to bestow upon them wisdom, insight, and a deep sense of humility as they fulfill their responsibilities and carry out their entrusted duties. May they be guided by your divine light in all their decisions and actions.

We pray that they may use their positions and influence for the betterment of the people under their care. Grant them the strength to stand against injustice, confront evil, eradicate corruption, defeat tyranny, break the chains of arrogance, and renounce ill-gotten gains. Let their leadership be a beacon of hope and justice for their nations.

Loving God, we implore you to soften their hearts and open them to the boundless grace found in Jesus' name. May they be vessels of compassion and understanding, working towards a world filled with peace, love, and harmony.

In your holy name, we offer these prayers, trusting in your infinite wisdom and grace. Amen.

PRAYER FOR THE WORKMEN

Heavenly Father,

As we stand in Your presence, we lift up in prayer all the workers around the world. From the dedicated police officers, military personnel, firefighters, ambulance paramedics, and nurses to the skilled midwives, diligent postmen, diligent shoppers, talented cooks, diligent cleaners, and all the artisans, craftsmen, performers, and service providers, we bring them before You.

Lord, we recognize that the world would be a vastly different place without these individuals and their unique talents. We are profoundly grateful for each one of them, for their contributions shape our daily lives.

We pray, Father God, that they may acknowledge You as the source of their gifts and talents. May they find joy and fulfillment in the callings they have embraced, knowing that their work serves a higher purpose.

Furthermore, Lord, we beseech You to fill their hearts with love and compassion as they carry out their tasks. May their efforts not only benefit themselves but also their families and communities. Grant them prosperity, both in material blessings and in the contentment that comes from knowing You are with them.

Thank You, Lord, for your watchful and guiding hand over them. In Your name, we offer these prayers, trusting in Your boundless love and grace. Amen.

Personal Prayer Guide

Use this page for your personal prayers and impressions. You can use this to write the names of people you are praying for and record testimonies of what God is doing through prayer.

CHAPTER 2

PRAYERS FOR FAMILIES AND PROTECTION

He came back to life

It was in the middle of the night, back in 2012, as I peacefully slumbered, that a remarkable dream unfolded. In this dream, a majestic lion approached me, its voice laden with challenge as it declared, "Between you and me, let us determine who truly stands as the victor." With unrelenting ferocity, it lunged toward me, its sharp claws and voracious teeth bared. The ensuing struggle left me feeling overwhelmed, as if I were losing the battle. In my desperation, I cried out, invoking the name of Jesus.

Suddenly, a transformation occurred. I felt the divine power of God surging within me, and I found myself soaring above the lion. Landing upon its back, I felt its spine yield under my touch. "You have triumphed!" the lion conceded, its roar echoing my victory.

In an instant, the words of Psalm 91 filled my senses, and then I awoke.

In the stillness of the night, an anguished cry pierced the silence from my neighbor's home. Without a second thought, I rose from my bed and hurried to their side. The mother's voice was a chorus of desperation as she wailed.

"What happened?" I inquired; my concern evident.

"He is dead," she gasped, her voice laden with grief.

Puzzled, I pressed for clarity, "Who?"

"My son," came her mournful reply.

"Could you bring him here?" I implored.

She complied, and as she brought her lifeless child to my doorstep, my heart sank. "Lay him down on the couch," I directed.

With trembling hands, she did as instructed. A solemn question hung in the air, "Shall I pray?" I ventured.

Her gaze met mine, a mixture of incredulity and despair. "What's your prayer going to do for him?" she questioned, skepticism etched across her face.

"I can pray if you're willing," I responded resolutely.

After a moment's hesitation, she relented, her voice defeated, "Just do it."

Turning my attention to the motionless child, I uttered a prayer with unwavering faith. "I command his spirit to return to this child," I declared. And then, in a breathtaking moment, I witnessed a subtle movement in the child's form. My prayer continued, and gradually, life returned to him, his eyes fluttering open as I restored him to his grateful mother.

It's worth noting that the mother adhered to a different faith and did not believe in Jesus. To my surprise, I later discovered that the child had worn a talisman of witchcraft around his waist. However, the healing touch of Jesus had made him whole once more!

PRAYER FOR FATHERS

Heavenly Father,

You are the Father of our Lord Jesus and the divine Father who dwells in Heaven. We lift our voices in praise of Your holy name. We recognize that being a father is a precious gift from You, and we come before You, earnestly praying that You grant every father the grace to fulfill their sacred role in accordance with Your original intent of fatherhood.

Dear fathers, today we unite in prayer, seeking God's blessings for you. We ask that God will:

- Fill your hearts with love, both for yourselves and your children.
- Grant you abundant patience to navigate the challenges of family life.
- Bestow upon you wisdom and intelligence to guide and support your children and wives.
- Open doors of opportunity so that you may provide for your families' needs.
- Empower you to lead your families in the ways of the Lord.
- Help you become the father figure every child longs to have.
- May your children see the reflection of God's love and grace in your actions.

We pray, Father, for the breaking of every yoke of trauma, stress, bondage, and addiction in the precious name of Jesus. We bestow upon all fathers the blessings of heaven and earth, invoking the name of Jesus upon them. Fathers, know that you are deeply loved.

In the name of our Lord and Savior, Jesus Christ, we offer these prayers, trusting in Your boundless love and grace. Amen.

PRAYER FOR MOTHERS

Heavenly Father,

We come before you with hearts full of gratitude for the mothers all around the world. We recognize that our existence is a testament to your divine plan, as you used these women to nurture and carry us for nine precious months. Their love for us even before our birth is a testament to your boundless love, Lord.

We thank you, Lord, for those mothers who are currently expecting new life within them. We pray for the blessings of increased love for their husbands and children. Grant them the gift of patience and inner peace as they care for the lives entrusted to them. May they be beacons of your teachings, dear Jesus, guiding their children along your path.

We lift up in prayer those mothers who may be trapped in anger, addiction, sexual immorality, and various forms of sin. In the name of Jesus, we pray for their deliverance from these chains. Release them from the grip of trauma, stress, and depression. Set them free, Lord, and renew their spirits.

May the fire of God's love be kindled within their hearts, revitalizing their inner strength and fortitude. To any mother who may not yet know the Lord, we extend this heartfelt invitation. Please close your eyes and invite Him into your life, for He stands before you, ready to love and save you. Your sins are no match for His love; He is here to forgive and liberate you from any bondage.

In the powerful name of Jesus, we break the chains of witchcraft and lies that have weighed heavy on your life. Mothers, know that you are cherished and blessed. Your light will shine brightly once more, and you will live to testify to the goodness of the Lord.

God takes immense pride in you, dear mothers. Now, take a moment to express your gratitude to God for your own mother and for all the other mothers whose lives have touched yours.

In Jesus' name, we offer these prayers, believing in your boundless love and grace. Amen.

I Want Your Head Beheaded

In the year 2000, I made a significant decision to change my path and embarked on a seminary course. During that time, I became entangled in a family dispute centered around religious matters. I signed a document agreeing to bear all the financial responsibilities for a woman and her child who were involved in the situation.

Fast forward to 2009, I found myself at home when I received threatening messages from the woman's father. He claimed that he would harm me within a month. In response, I calmly reminded him that if he had the power to put my life in danger, then he had the authority to take it away. However, if he didn't possess control over my life, he had no right to threaten me in such a manner.

In the midst of this challenging situation, I decided to set aside everything for seven days to seek comfort and guidance from God. During this period, I even chose to sleep on the floor as a symbol of my earnestness. I poured my heart out to the Lord, beseeching His intervention in my life. Miraculously, the Lord answered my prayers and delivered me from the impending danger. What I experienced during that time transcended my comprehension, as I couldn't fully grasp the extent of His intervention.

Several weeks later, to my surprise, I learned that the individual who had issued the threat, a man of my age, had tragically passed away in his sleep. This event marked a profound loss for their family, leaving me reflecting on the inexplicable events that had unfolded

DAY 6

PRAYER FOR SINGLE PARENTS

Heavenly Father,

Today, we come before you with hearts full of compassion, lifting up single parents in our prayers. We thank you for them, for the incredible strength and resilience they demonstrate each day. We can only imagine the challenges they face as they strive to fulfill the roles of both mother and father.

Lord, we pray for your sustaining grace to envelop them during these times. Grant them the strength they need, along with an abundance of love, patience, and inner peace as they care for the precious lives you have entrusted to their care.

Help them understand that having a child is a blessing and not a burden, dear Lord. Open their eyes to the beauty and joy found in their journey as parents.

Father, meet all their needs—emotional, physical, and spiritual. Shower them with provisions from above, ensuring they lack nothing.

May they perceive your guiding hand and unfailing love in their lives. Restore their spirits, lift them from the dust and ashes, and let their light shine once more.

In the name of Jesus, we break the chains of depression and stress that weigh heavy on their shoulders. Replace their burdens with your peace and strength, dear Lord.

We hear your comforting words, Lord, as you assure them, "You are not alone. I am with you." In Jesus' name, we bless them. And to those who may not yet know you, we invite them to open their hearts and invite you in, for you are faithful and patient in forgiving sins and transgressions. Remind them that they are deeply loved.

In gratitude, we offer praise to you, Lord. We also lift up two or three single parents we know and pray for them in your mighty name. Amen.

He Keeps Me from The Grave

In the year 1989, I was a student in standard two at Irambo Primary School. One fateful day, as I was returning home from school, having already covered about half of the eight-mile journey, an unusual and unsettling incident occurred. I noticed a motorbike approaching me, and it came to a sudden halt right in front of me.

A mysterious figure, his face obscured by a veil, approached me. Despite my attempts to evade him, he managed to grab hold of me, rendering me immobile. To my shock and horror, he reached into his pocket and produced a pistol, pointing it menacingly at my face. As he was on the verge of pulling the trigger, a powerful force abruptly overcame me, causing me to collapse at his feet.

In his haste, he inadvertently trampled over me and hastily retreated, assuming that I had fled in fear. He even returned briefly, still agitated, and unknowingly trampled over me again as he searched for any sign of my escape. Perplexed by my sudden disappearance, he eventually abandoned his sinister intentions and continued on his way.

It was only afterward that I began to comprehend the events of that day. I realized that it was the divine hand of God that shielded me from the malevolent intentions of the assailant, concealing me from his sight and sparing my life. Moreover, that same divine intervention lifted me to my feet once the danger had passed, although, at the time, my understanding of these miraculous events was limited due to my spiritual immaturity.

The Bible says in the book of Psalms 103:4 (GNB):
"Bless the Lord, my soul!
All my being blesses his holy name!
Praise the Lord, my soul
And do not forget how kind he is.
He forgives all my sins and heals all my diseases.
HE KEEPS MY LIFE FROM THE GRAVE
And blesses me with love and mercy."

I have personally witnessed the fulfillment of this scripture in my life: the Lord rescued me from the clutches of a deadly adversary. It was undeniably a close call, and it seemed as though my time on this earth was drawing to a perilous end. However, I am profoundly grateful to God, for delivering us from the brink of destruction is one of His divine acts of mercy.

Death manifests in two distinct forms: physical death, marked by the cessation of our mortal breath, and spiritual death, which ensues when we lead lives steeped in sin. Spiritual death occurs when we unwittingly open the door to this perilous state through our actions.

In the Garden of Eden, God warned Adam that partaking of the forbidden fruit would lead to death. This, however, was a reference to spiritual death, signifying the loss of our godly connection and a glimpse of humanity's grim destiny—eternal separation in the abyss of hell.

We are eternally grateful for the intervention of Jesus, for He came to grant us life, and not just any life, but life in abundance and fullness.

PRAYER FOR OUR TEACHERS

Teaching is an enduring endeavor that leaves an everlasting imprint on young souls. You shoulder a delicate responsibility, for the children within your classroom are like clay in the hands of a skilled potter, and your classroom is the potter's house. It is within your power to mold and shape these lives.

Today, we join together in prayer, seeking the divine guidance and strength necessary for you to fulfill your calling faithfully. Our first petition is that God fills your hearts with His boundless love, enabling you to handle your students with tenderness and care. May the time these students spend in your classroom be marked by the indelible imprints of love and compassion.

We beseech the Almighty to grant you wisdom beyond the confines of your educational curriculum. May you not only impart knowledge but also impart the invaluable wisdom that transcends the boundaries of the classroom. May the Lord safeguard you from inadvertently leading these young lives astray amidst the falsehoods of the world.

In Jesus' name, we fervently pray for your liberation from any falsehoods that may cast shadows over your life. May the Lord, in His infinite grace, free you from the clutches of insecurity or depression, allowing you to embrace life to the fullest.

With deep admiration and respect for your vital role, we offer these prayers for your continued strength, wisdom, and fulfillment in shaping the future generations. Amen.

Personal Prayer Guide

Use this page for your personal prayers and impressions. You can use this to write the names of people you are praying for and record testimonies of what God is doing through prayer.

CHAPTER 3

PRAYER TO STRENGHTEN FAITH

As A Man Thinketh, So Is He

'Believing' is the profound act of embracing something as true and anchoring faith and confidence in it. This form of belief allows individuals to perceive the world not solely through their physical senses, but through the lens of inner vision, which I often refer to as faith. The Bible provides a beautiful definition, stating that *"faith is the assurance of things hoped for, the conviction of things not seen"* (Hebrews 11:1 ESV).

In essence, faith transcends the tangible and empowers individuals to trust in the unseen, to hope for the unrealized, and to have unwavering confidence in divine promises. It is a force that fuels the human spirit, enabling us to navigate life's uncertainties and challenges with resilience and a profound sense of purpose.

This story brings to mind an experience with a dear friend of mine. Back in 1993, during my uncle's wedding celebration, our family hosted a grand feast. It was a joyous occasion, and everyone indulged in the sumptuous spread. However, my friend and I were still quite young at the time, and he noticed something peculiar.

As we savored the meal, we encountered some tough pieces of meat that were challenging to chew due to their muscular texture. In his innocence, my friend turned to me and said, "Please don't discard those pieces. I want to eat them so I can grow muscles like a cow!"

Amused by his request, we handed over the meat, and he eagerly devoured it. We couldn't help but wait, expecting to witness his transformation into a muscular figure resembling a cow. To our surprise, nothing extraordinary happened at the time.

Fast forward to 2014, I had the opportunity to reunite with my friend. What I saw left me astounded. His arms, legs, and neck had indeed developed an unusual level of muscularity, resembling that of a cow. It was a striking visual reminder of his earlier belief in the power of consuming cow's muscles for growth—a belief that had astonishingly come to fruition.

In the book of Romans 10:8, we find a powerful principle: "But what does it say? 'The word is near you, in your mouth and in your heart' (that is, the word of faith that we proclaim); because, if you confess with your mouth that Jesus is Lord and believe in your heart that God raised him from the dead, you will be saved."

To confess, in this context, means to wholeheartedly agree with a specific truth. In the case of salvation, it means acknowledging Jesus as Lord and accepting the profound truth of His resurrection by God. Just as my friend saw his muscles grow through his belief, the moment we confess Jesus as Lord, our salvation, though expressed in the future, begins at that very instant. This truth parallels the transformative power of faith, enabling us to step into a new life of eternal significance. You can only become what you believe.

PRAYER FOR THE AMBULANCE DRIVERS AND PARAMEDICS

Heavenly Father,

As we embark on this new day, we lift our hearts to You, seeking Your blessings upon those who serve as ambulance drivers and paramedics. We beseech You to shower them with joy, boldness, strength, and love as they step out to fulfill their vital roles.

We recall the words of Lamentations 3:21-23: *"But this I call to mind; therefore, I have hope. It is because of the Lord's loving-kindnesses that we are not consumed, because His tender compassions never fail. They are new every morning; great and beyond measure is Your faithfulness."* Your mercies are renewed every morning, and for this, we are profoundly grateful.

Lord, we pray that You guide their hands and words as they minister to those in need, in the precious name of Jesus. May these blessings overflow into their families as well. We entrust them into Your care throughout the day, Lord, and ask that Your divine light shines brilliantly within their hearts as they go about their daily duties.

In gratitude and humility, we open our hearts to You, Lord Jesus, inviting You to walk alongside us. Just as Psalm 121:8 proclaims, *"The Lord will watch over your coming and going both now and forevermore,"* we place our trust in Your unwavering protection.

We acknowledge our shortcomings and humbly ask for Your forgiveness. Be our Lord and Savior, and in surrender, we offer ourselves to You completely. Fill us with Your Holy Spirit, lead us in Your ways, and know that we love You dearly.

Now, in this moment, let us pause to lift up in prayer a paramedic we know personally. With heartfelt gratitude, we thank You for each one of them. In the mighty and compassionate name of Jesus, we bestow blessings upon them all. Amen.

PRAYER FOR REFUGEES

Heavenly Father,

In the midst of the turmoil that has befallen regions like Ukraine, Congo, Nigeria, and the Middle East, countless souls have been forced to flee their homes and seek refuge in unfamiliar lands.

Gracious Father, we lift our prayers on behalf of these refugees, knowing that You stand with them in their time of need. Your word teaches us in Psalm 34:18 that *"The Lord is near to the brokenhearted and saves the crushed in spirit."* We implore You to reunite those who have been separated from their families, to help them adapt to their new circumstances, and to illuminate their lives with Your light, love, and mercy.

Lord, we beseech You to call those who do not yet know You, for Your grace is boundless, and Your love knows no bounds. In Ezekiel 11:19-20, You promise, *"And I will give them one heart, and a new spirit I will put within them. I will remove the heart of stone from their flesh and give them a heart of flesh."* We pray that You perform this divine transformation in their lives.

May any trauma, depression, or stress caused by their harrowing experiences be shattered in the mighty name of Jesus. Your word assures us in Isaiah 41:10, "Fear not, for I am with you; be not dismayed, for I am your God; I will strengthen you, I will help you, I will uphold you with my righteous right hand."

Lord, help them find comfort in the knowledge that Jesus, too, was once a refugee, fleeing with His family. He understands their plight intimately and offers unwavering support. We remind them that they can always count on Him, for He has their backs.

For those who have not yet welcomed Jesus into their hearts, we extend this invitation. Close your eyes, and invite Him in, for He is knocking at the door of your heart. Open it to Him, and He will dine with you today. Offer gratitude for His salvation and His lordship over your life, for you are now a beloved child of God.

Let us also take a moment to lift up in prayer three to five people we know who are displaced, standing in solidarity with them. May they find strength, comfort, and renewed hope in You, O Lord.

In Jesus' name, we pray for peace, healing, and restoration. Amen.

PRAYER FOR THOSE IN PRISON

"When you lie down, you will not be afraid; Yes, you will lie down and your sleep will be sweet. Do not be afraid of sudden terror, Nor of trouble from the wicked when it comes." (Proverbs 3:24-25)

Heavenly Father,

Today, we come together in prayer, lifting our hearts for those who find themselves in difficult circumstances. We may not fully understand why they are where they are, but we pray for them with unwavering hope and compassion.

Lord, we beseech You to remind them that they are not alone, for Your presence knows no bounds. Your word assures us in Isaiah 41:10, *"Fear not, for I am with you; be not dismayed, for I am your God; I will strengthen you, I will help you, I will uphold you with my righteous right hand."* We pray that during their journey, like a caterpillar undergoing metamorphosis, they emerge transformed, their beauty shining brightly.

May the radiant light of Christ shine within their hearts, bringing them comfort and hope. We pray that they encounter Your boundless love, for You identify with them intimately. In Matthew 25:36, Your word reminds us that, *"I was in prison and you came to me."* They are not alone, for You are with them, walking beside them in their trials.

For those who have yet to open their hearts to You, Lord, we extend an invitation. May they discover Your love, the love that led You to sacrifice Your life for them. We pray that they embrace this divine opportunity.

We earnestly implore You, O God, to fill them with Your Holy Spirit. Break every yoke that burdens their shoulders – addiction, trauma, despair, and falsehoods. In Jesus' mighty name, we declare these bonds broken, for You are the ultimate source of liberation.

Let the freedom of the Lord wash over them. May every sleepless night give way to peaceful rest, as Proverbs 3:24-25 proclaims: *"If you lie down, you will not be afraid; when you lie down, your sleep will be sweet. Do not be afraid of sudden terror or of the ruin of the wicked when it comes."*

We pray for fairness and grace during their trials, and we trust in Your providence, Lord. May Your blessings flow over them, spiritually and physically, leading them out of their current circumstances.

Now, let us take a moment to intercede for other inmates, naming those we know and expecting the saving and liberating grace of God to touch their lives.

In Jesus' name, we pray for transformation, freedom, and salvation. Amen

PRAYER FOR FIREFIGHTERS

"Even though I walk through the [sunless] valley of the shadow of death, I fear no evil, for You are with me; Your rod [to protect] and Your staff [to guide], they comfort and console me". (Psalm 23:4)

"When you pass through the waters; I will be with you; And through the rivers, they will not overwhelm you. When you walk through fire, you will not be scorched, nor will the flame burn you." (Isaiah 43:2)

Heavenly Father,

Your word assures us in Isaiah 43:2 that when we pass through the fires, we will not be consumed, and when we traverse deep waters, they will not overwhelm us. Today, we come before You, lifting up those who find themselves in the midst of trials and tribulations, including bushfires, building fires, and other challenges.

We pray for their safety and strength, both spiritually and physically. May Your divine protection surround them, O Lord, as they navigate through these fiery ordeals. Grant them the resilience to withstand the heat and turmoil they face.

In the words of Numbers 6:24-26, we invoke Your blessings upon them: *"The Lord bless you and keep you; the Lord make his face to shine upon you and be gracious to you; the Lord lift up his countenance upon you and give you peace."* They are indeed doing a sacred work of salvation.

Our heartfelt prayer is that they come to know the boundless love of our Savior, Jesus Christ. Just as He willingly walked through the fires of this world to rescue us, may they encounter His deep and abiding love today. We fervently pray for their mental health, asking that every trace of trauma, depression, and stress be shattered in the mighty name of Jesus.

We remind them, Lord, not to fear, for You are with them. As Your word in Isaiah 41:10 reassures us, *"Fear not, for I am with you; be not dismayed, for I am your God; I will strengthen you, I will help you, I will uphold you with my righteous right hand."* May this truth fill their hearts with courage and faith.

In Jesus' name, we offer this prayer, trusting in Your unwavering presence and protection.

Amen.

Use this page for your personal prayers and impressions. You can use this to write the names of people you are praying for and record testimonies of what God is doing through prayer.

CHAPTER 4

PRAYERS FOR HEALING

Miraculous Healing

The Bible says in Psalms 103:3b, *"..Who heals all your disease?"*

The truth is, forgiveness plays a profound role in our spiritual and physical wholeness, as the apostle Paul beautifully articulates in the Corinthians. When we embrace Christ, our past is swept away, and we are reborn as new creations, with everything transformed into a glorious newness.

I vividly recall the day I surrendered my life to Jesus, a moment that forever altered my existence. At the time, I was grappling with a debilitating ailment that had left me almost handicapped. I had exhausted every possible medical remedy, yet none had brought relief.

Then came that September Sunday when I reluctantly attended church. As I watched the congregation fervently praising the Lord, I couldn't help but find their expressions a bit perplexing. An inner voice persisted, urging me to surrender my life to Jesus, but I resisted its persistent call.

During the pastor's sermon, an overwhelming conviction overcame me, compelling me to rise and declare, "I want to give my life to Jesus." The congregation rallied around me in prayer, and from that day forward, I dedicated my life to Christ. In a miraculous turn of events, the Lord graciously healed my agonizing affliction.

A scripture that resonates deeply with me is the one that encourages us to "seek the kingdom of God first, and all things will be added unto us." It serves as a powerful reminder of God's promise to provide for His faithful children.

To God, the ultimate healer, be all the glory!

Take Her to Church

In our small church nestled in the quiet corner of our community, we faithfully gathered each morning, beginning at five forty-five and often extending our fellowship well into the morning hours.

One particular morning, I awoke and embarked on my daily 8.4-kilometer journey to the church. Upon my arrival, I was joined by a fellow brother and sister, forming a small congregation ready to celebrate the glorious morning together.

As we engaged in prayer, the tangible presence of the Lord enveloped us. Suddenly, our sacred assembly was interrupted by a great commotion emanating from our corner of the world. The words, "Take her to church," resounded in our ears.

Before us was a young girl, motionless and struggling for breath. She was Liz, although that name is merely a pseudonym. It's worth noting that Liz was not a regular member of our church, despite residing nearby. On this particular morning, she had risen early to fetch water, a precious commodity in Goma, often likened to the rarity of diamonds. Consequently, residents would go to great lengths to secure their place in line at the water source.

Liz had succeeded in securing water ahead of others but suddenly collapsed while attempting to carry her jerrycan. Gasping for air, she was quickly carried to our humble church in the corner by those who had been waiting their turn at the tap.

Liz lay before us, her life hanging in the balance. An elder approached me, expressing his desire to interview her and understand what had transpired. "She is dying," I remarked, "what answers do you expect from her?" Instead, we turned to fervent prayer, rebuking the spirit of death that had taken hold of her. I distinctly recall the aggressive resistance of this malevolent spirit within her.

Nonetheless, no spirit can prevail against the mighty name of Jesus, for as the Word of God assures us, "Every knee shall bow." And so, it came to pass.

By the end of that day, the spirit of death had departed, and Liz was set free. Slowly, she returned to life, regaining her faculties. While she was undoubtedly fatigued, she also felt refreshed and liberated. I sat down with her, eager to learn about her harrowing experience.

Liz recounted, "A man approached me and declared his intention to take my life. Suddenly, he reached out towards my heart, and I fell. After that, I remember nothing until I found myself here in the church."

Brethren, Liz had experienced a miraculous deliverance. Death, with all its menacing power, was rendered powerless before the name of Jesus.

In our moments of deepest distress, we must always remember that Jesus reigns supreme, triumphant over every force that seeks to steal life and hope from us.

DAY 12

PRAYER FOR THE SICK

"Call on Me in the day of trouble; I will rescue you, and you shall honor and glorify Me." (Psalm 50:15)

"Is anyone among you sick? He must call for the elders (spiritual leaders) of the church and they are to pray over him, anointing him with oil in the name of the Lord." (James 5:14)

Heavenly Father,

Today, we come before You on behalf of those who are suffering from illness, whether at home or in the hospital. We recognize that You are Jehovah Rapha, the Healer, for You are our God and their God. In the name of Jesus, we lift our prayers, asking for Your divine touch.

We fervently pray that every sickness be cast away in the powerful name of Jesus. We break every possible power and spirit of infirmity that may be afflicting them. In Luke 4:18, Jesus proclaims, "The Spirit of the Lord is upon me because he has anointed me to proclaim good news to the poor. He has sent me to proclaim liberty to the captives and recovering of sight to the blind, to set at liberty those who are oppressed." May Your liberating power be unleashed upon them now.

We rebuke every evil spirit that may be behind their pain in their bowels, backbone, and joints, casting it out in Jesus' name. We command every heart disease to cease its progression and vanish from their bodies, aligning with Your divine will.

For those battling diabetes, we rebuke this condition in the mighty name of Jesus. We pray for the peace of the Lord to permeate their bodies, hearts, and minds, bringing comfort and healing.

Cancer, we speak against you with authority. Release your grip from their bones, blood, and bodies, for they are beloved children of God. We declare healing and restoration in the name of Jesus.

Father, we ask for Your forgiveness for any sins in their lives, knowing that Your love is boundless. We pray that Your love be revealed to them at this very moment. In the powerful name of Jesus, we break every suicidal thought and desire, replacing them with Your peace and hope.

We thank You, Lord, for Your mercies and healing touch. In Jesus' name, we offer this prayer, believing in Your transformative power and grace.

Amen.

Set aside a moment to recall someone you know, and witness the Lord's healing grace upon them. Read and reflect upon Psalm 50:15 and Isaiah 53:5.

Dann Healed from Epilepsy

In the year 2006, nestled within the humble confines of a small house, a tiny church known as the "little church in the corner" thrived. It was home to a family with four children, including a young boy named Dann, who silently battled epilepsy.

Despite the modest surroundings, this little church blazed with a fervent love for Jesus, and extraordinary things unfolded within its four wooden walls. The faithful congregants, though financially challenged, possessed an unwavering faith in the greatness of God.

Dann's mother brought him to the church for prayer, seeking divine intervention for her son's severe epilepsy. Their prayers rose ceaselessly, and as a year passed, many anticipated the inevitable collapse of young Dann. However, the Lord had a different plan; He touched Dann's life, and miraculously, he was completely healed. The epilepsy that had plagued him since age seven vanished into oblivion.

I recently had the privilege of visiting Dann, and his remarkable health, and strength astounded me. He had blossomed into a talented singer, proficient in playing various musical instruments, and even a songwriter. Dann was whole and serving the Lord with a joyful heart. Truly, praise be to the Lord!

The Bible recounts the story of an epileptic boy who fell into dreadful convulsions but found healing and wholeness in the presence of Jesus. Dann's experience mirrors this divine intervention, and it serves as a powerful testament to the healing touch of the Lord. If you carry a burden of illness or affliction, bring your case before the Lord and trust in His miraculous healing power. He is still in the business of healing, just as He was in the days of Luke 9:40-44:

"But even while the boy was on his way, the spirit hurled him to the ground in a dreadful convulsion. Then Jesus reprimanded the evil spirit, healed the lad, and handed him back to his father. And it amazed everybody present at this demonstration of the power of God."

DAY 13

PRAYER FOR NURSES IN HOSPITALS

"But when he, the Spirit of truth, comes, he will guide you into all the truth. He will not speak on his own; he will speak only what he hears, and he will tell you what is yet to come." John 16:13

Heavenly Father,

Today, we lift up our friend who is heading to work, where her hands will touch the sick. We ask for Your divine guidance and intervention as she fulfills her calling. We pray that when her hands touch the sick, they may convey Your loving and healing touch in the name of Jesus.

Guard her mind, Lord, and shield it from the trauma that may result from what she witnesses. Grant her wisdom when she encounters complex situations, and illuminate the path she should follow.

May her words be guided by Your Spirit, that she may speak with grace, compassion, and timeliness to those she encounters. Protect her heart, for it is the wellspring of life. Fill her with Your love and compassion each day as she walks in her calling. Encounter her daily, O God, and pour out Your grace upon her.

We pray for physical strength for those who may be tired and experiencing burnout. Revive and regenerate them by Your Holy Spirit, Lord.

In the name of Jesus, we break every spirit of numbness that may seek to hinder their work. We rebuke any addiction that may hold them captive and shackle them. We command these chains to be broken in Jesus' name. We also dispel any falsehoods that may cloud their lives, asking for Your truth to prevail. May the Spirit of the Lord lead them into all truth, guiding their steps and granting them discernment. In John 16:13, Jesus promised, *"When the Spirit of truth comes, he will guide you into all the truth."* We claim this promise for our friend.

In the name of Jesus, we offer this prayer, trusting in Your boundless grace and mercy.

Amen.

Personal Prayer Guide

Use this page for your personal prayers and impressions. You can use this to write the names of people you are praying for and record testimonies of what God is doing through prayer.

CHAPTER 5

PRAYERS FOR SALVATION

A Hater Becomes a Friend

In the year 2010, when the Lord called upon me to journey to Uganda and proclaim the good news of His peace, I had the privilege of visiting the EPC church for the very first time. It was during this visit that the Lord imparted a powerful message to me, one that would become the theme of my sermon for the church congregation. The message was simply, "REMEMBER," and it drew its inspiration from the book of Revelation 2:5.

> *"Remember therefore whence thou art fallen, and repent, and do the first works; or else I will come unto thee quickly, and will remove thy candlestick out of his place, except thou repent."*

For a week, I passionately preached this message, and the response from the people was nothing short of exhilarating. They expressed their gratitude to the Lord for sending this message to them, and I rejoiced in the souls that turned to the Lord in repentance.

However, amidst the congregation, there was a lady who had attended the church while I was delivering the sermon. By God's grace, the Lord granted me a word for her, a word of salvation. Initially, she found it hard to believe, not because the message was inaccurate but because she held a deep-seated resentment towards me. However, the prophetic word I had shared with her eventually came to pass.

In due course, this lady extended an invitation to meet and talk with her. Her words were frank and revealing. "Roland, I want you to understand something today. The first time I saw you, I despised you immensely," she confessed. "Even on the day you preached and delivered God's message to me, my hatred for you remained strong. Deep down in my heart, I couldn't deny that God had used you to convey His truth."

She continued, "Yes, you became a source of help to me in various ways, and now I am humbly repenting before you."

I discerned that she was tormented by a malevolent spiritual presence, and the Lord had orchestrated her salvation through our encounter. I also understood that her previous actions were driven by the manifestation of this evil spirit within her. Consequently, the Lord granted me the strength to pray fervently for her and provide encouragement until she experienced complete deliverance.

Over time, she not only became a dear and genuine friend but also played a pivotal role in leading several members of her own family to Jesus through her transformed life.

Glory to God for His wondrous works and redemptive power!

PRAYER FOR NON-CHRISTIANS

"But He was wounded for our transgressions, He was crushed for our wickedness [our sin, our injustice, our wrongdoing]; The punishment [required] for our well-being fell on Him, And by His stripes (wounds) we are healed."(Isaiah 53:5)

"Therefore, let everyone who is godly pray to You [for forgiveness] in a time when You [are near and] may be found; Surely when the great waters [of trial and distressing times] overflow, they will not reach [the spirit in] him." Psalms 32:6

Heavenly Father,

Your boundless love knows no limits, and Your desire is that none should perish. Today, we come before You in prayer, interceding for our dear friend who has not yet embraced Your Son, Jesus Christ.

We pray for our friend, that their eyes may be opened to see the light, just as Paul did on his transformative journey. May a divine light shine not only in their physical eyes but also in the eyes of their heart. We earnestly seek this revelation for them. Today, Lord, may they hear Your voice calling them, beckoning them to come closer, just as You promised in John 10:27: *"My sheep hear my voice, and I know them, and they follow me."*

May they understand that their sins, no matter how great, are not greater than Your boundless love and grace. Your grace surrounds them even as they read these words. We extend the gift of God to them today, inviting them to accept it with open hearts. In this moment, Lord, may they choose to embrace the gift of Your Son, Jesus Christ.

Thank You, Father, for the transformation that has taken place as our friend accepts Jesus into their life. We rejoice that they are now Your child.

We pray for divine protection over their life from this day forward. May they be filled with Your Holy Spirit and used mightily in Your service. We offer our gratitude, Lord, for this wonderful transformation.

In the precious name of Jesus, we pray. Amen.

I Saw Jesus in Your Eyes

This remarkable event unfolded on a Wednesday evening at the church in Pemba back in the year 2015. Each Wednesday evening, we held a church gathering starting at 6:30 p.m., and it was mandatory for all the Harvest School students to attend. As expected, we were all present that evening, and the atmosphere was charged with spiritual anticipation.

As the service drew to a close, an extraordinary sight caught my attention. A sizable crowd of students suddenly rushed to the altar, leaving me intrigued and wondering, "What's happening here?" It soon became apparent that the guest, a speaker visiting from the USA, had instructed all the students to form a line. They obediently lined up, and he, along with his wife, began praying for them. To my astonishment, many of these students fell prostrate on the floor under the power of the Spirit.

While this captivating scene unfolded, I remained seated on the stair bench. Gradually, almost everyone left the church building. However, I felt an unmistakable presence of God's glory right where I was seated, compelling me to stay a while longer.

Suddenly, a young man approached me, shook my hand vigorously, and exclaimed, "Man, what's happening here?" He closed his eyes, then reopened them, gazed at me for a moment, and walked away in deep contemplation.

My heart remained tethered to the tangible presence of God in that very spot. Eventually, I sensed the Spirit's gentle leading, prompting me to move toward the altar. Following His guidance,

I approached E.L, who was lying on the floor in an intense encounter with God. I laid my hands upon him, touching his legs, stomach, and hands. As I prayed, a profound sense of peace washed over him, and he grew still. I embraced him and spoke words of blessing and affirmation over his life.

But the divine encounters did not end there. I cast my gaze across the room and noticed three ladies. I felt an inner prompting to approach one of them, Mel. As I laid my hands on her, an extraordinary occurrence unfolded. Mel fixed her eyes upon me, and suddenly, she burst into uncontrollable laughter. She rolled on the floor, overwhelmed by joy, unable to contain her mirth.

The following evening, during our night worship session, Mallorie sought me out with eager anticipation. She shared her profound experience from the previous night's church service. "I've been told stories back home about people encountering Jesus in person in Africa," she began. Her eyes sparkled with hope as she continued, "But last night, it happened to me. When I shook your hand and looked into your eyes, I saw Jesus in your eyes. It was an incredible moment, my first personal encounter with Him."

Such encounters serve as a powerful reminder of the extraordinary presence and grace of our Lord Jesus Christ, manifesting in ways that continue to inspire and transform lives.

On January 18, 2016, she sent me a personal message via Facebook. This is what she wrote:

Hi Rolland!

Happy New Year too!! It's so good to hear from you!

The other day I remembered when we were at Harvest School and when the Lord answered my prayer of what it meant to see Him in someone like literally see Him. And then one night after Wednesday church, when a lot [of] us were praying for each other, I opened my eyes and looked at you, and I just kept literally seeing Jesus in your eyes and face, and it was just so cool! (Haha) the Lord just like blew me away when He did that! I was just completely in awe of Jesus when He did this! (Haha) It was awesome, but I thought I would share that with you because it was so amazing!

But anyway, Happy New Year, and I pray you are doing well in the Lord!!

I am deeply rejuvenated by the touch of His grace, and it is with great honor that I share this remarkable experience in Pemba with all who read these words.

Our journey into this extraordinary encounter began with our customary Friday activity known as Mercy Ministry. Every Friday, we embarked on a mission to construct a home for a Mozambican family. This noble endeavor required us to carry sacks of sand, cement, bricks, and various construction materials.

As the clock ticked toward the appointed hour on that particular Friday, our task shifted to transporting bricks, cement, sand, and paint containers to the construction site. It was a laborious but fulfilling undertaking, and we faithfully executed our duties, even if it meant that we had to continue the work into the following day.

However, an unexpected challenge presented itself. As we assessed the construction site, we realized that a crucial element was missing—a restroom. In response, we were tasked with digging a pit latrine, and this was no ordinary task. The ground proved unyielding, its hardness resisting our every effort.

Our determined group of workers, undeterred by the unforgiving earth, began the arduous process of digging a pit latrine, a task that would require us to excavate to a depth of three meters. The physical strain was undeniable, but we pressed on, knowing that this mission was not just about constructing a house but also about creating a home, a place where a family would find shelter, comfort, and a sense of belonging.

In times like these, I am reminded of the words of Psalm 127:1 (ESV): *"Unless the Lord builds the house, those who build it labor in vain."* Our labor was infused with a greater purpose, an understanding that even as we toiled with bricks and mortar, we were part of a divine construction project—one that built not only physical structures but also lasting hope, love, and transformation in the lives of those we served.

So, with every shovel of earth we turned, we were not merely digging a pit but also digging deep into the hearts of the Mozambican people, sowing seeds of compassion, and cultivating the fertile soil of faith. In the end, we knew that our efforts, fueled by His touch, would yield a harvest of blessings far beyond what we could see or imagine.

PRAYER FOR GOD'S FORGIVENESS

Heavenly Father,

In Your presence, I find comfort, knowing that You are always attentive to my voice. I confess that my life has been marked by mistakes and imperfections, often feeling unworthy of Your boundless love and forgiveness. Yet, in Your grace, You have come to me, and for this, I am profoundly grateful.

With a heart humbled by Your mercy, I surrender myself to You. I ask for Your forgiveness, Lord, for all my sins and transgressions. May You cleanse me from the stains of my past and make me pure.

I swing open the door of my heart, inviting You, Lord Jesus, to become the guiding light of my life, my Lord and Savior from this moment onward.

Dear God, I embrace You as my Father, recognizing my identity as Your child. I am overwhelmed with gratitude for Your forgiveness and unwavering love.

As I lift my prayers to You, I also intercede on behalf of two or three seniors I know. I thank You, Lord, for the precious gift of salvation in their lives and ask that Your blessings continue to overflow in their hearts.

In Jesus' name, I offer this prayer, strengthened by Your grace and inspired by Your Word.

Amen.

Personal Prayer Guide

Use this page for your personal prayers and impressions. You can use this to write the names of people you are praying for and record testimonies of what God is doing through prayer.

CHAPTER 6

PRAYERS FOR GOD'S HELP

Physical appearance deceives!

The Lord empowered me to assist Elisabeth, a sister in faith, with various matters. She had siblings who were previously unfamiliar with the Lord, and she chose to introduce them to me.

Upon arriving at Elisabeth's home, I had the pleasure of meeting her sister, Kiza. However, to my surprise, Elisabeth greeted me in their local dialect with the words, "Pasta kali book," which loosely translated to "The pastor is still a baby" or "Baby pastor."

I couldn't help but be taken aback by this seemingly judgmental remark. After all, I was thirty-one years old at the time, and her words stung. However, little did I know that this encounter would serve as a profound lesson about the boundless power of God.

As our conversation unfolded, the Lord began to open my eyes, and I felt compelled to share insights about Elisabeth's life that I couldn't have known otherwise. She was deeply moved and began to weep. It became evident that God's transformative power transcends age and physical appearance.

Elisabeth had been married to a witch doctor and had a child with him. However, when the divine touch of God reached her heart, she made a life-altering decision. She turned her back on her previous religious beliefs in Islam and wholeheartedly embraced Jesus Christ as her Lord and Savior. Following her conversion, she underwent baptism as a public declaration of her faith.

Her journey, however, was far from smooth. Elisabeth had accumulated a substantial bank loan, exceeding fourteen million Ugandan shillings (equivalent to US$5,100), and she was at a loss about how to repay it. In desperation, she had turned to witch doctors for a solution, but the debt still loomed over her.

Then came a remarkable encounter when we crossed paths again. Through God's miraculous intervention, the loan was miraculously paid off, and a burden was lifted from her shoulders. I took this opportunity to lovingly advise her not to take out any more loans from the bank. Regrettably, she did not heed this counsel and ended up borrowing three million Ugandan shillings.

When I returned to Uganda in December 2013, our paths crossed once more. Elisabeth's eyes welled up with tears as she expressed gratitude for my return. It was then that she shared her distressing predicament: she was on the brink of a crisis due to the new loan.

In our conversation, she admitted her lapse, saying, "I am sorry. I know you advised against it, but I couldn't resist the temptation. Now, I don't know how to repay it."

In God's boundless mercy, we joined our hearts in prayer, seeking divine intervention. I also reached out to the church pastor, and together we fervently prayed for Elisabeth's deliverance from this financial burden. To our amazement and joy, our prayers were answered—the loan was miraculously cleared, and Elisabeth was set free to pursue her own business endeavors.

This powerful testimony serves as a testament to God's unwavering grace and transformative power. Even when we stumble and make mistakes, His mercy abounds, providing solutions to our most daunting challenges and guiding us toward a brighter future.

PRAYER FOR FAMILIES

Heavenly Father,

Today, I stand before Your throne, bringing before You all the families across the globe. We thank You, Lord, for the godly families that exist, a testament to Your grace and love.

On this day, we lift our prayers for every family, asking for the abundance of peace, joy, love, and celebration to fill their homes.

For those families enduring difficult times, marked by struggles like divorce, separation, sickness, loss, debt, bankruptcy, famine, and suffering, we beseech You, Lord, to provide comfort, provision, and breakthrough in the mighty name of Jesus. May Your healing touch mend what is broken and restore what is lost.

Lord, we humbly ask for Your love and power, which have the extraordinary ability to break the yokes that burden families.

We fervently pray that every family on this Earth becomes a sanctuary where Your presence is welcomed daily. May they share the bread of life, birth missions within their homes, release the gifts of the Spirit, witness the growth of the fruits of the Spirit, and become the epicenters of revival.

Thank You, Father, for providing homes to those without one, and for guiding wayward sons back to their families, just as the prodigal son was welcomed with open arms.

In the name of Jesus, we offer this prayer, believing in Your transformative power and the miracles You can work in every family's life.

Amen.

Lord, I am grateful that this is the moment when You are reuniting the hearts of fathers with their children and sons with their fathers. May Your name be glorified, Lord, in the name of Jesus.

PRAYER FOR THE HOMELESS

Heavenly Father,

We come before You with heavy hearts, mindful of the many people who are in search of a home, often finding themselves sleeping on the streets, alongside roads, and under bridges. Today, we lift them up in prayer.

We implore You, Father God, to provide them with a place to call home. Break away from their lives the sense of abandonment and the weight of curses that may have haunted them.

For You, Lord, are a God of love, and we pray that You pour out Your love upon them. May they receive Your love and embrace it fully, casting aside anything that causes them to wander aimlessly.

In the powerful name of Jesus, we command every falsehood that has hung over their lives to fall away. We thank You, Lord, for a new home that You will provide for them. We praise You for sending help from Heaven to meet their needs.

As we pray together, we ask that each of them open their hearts and receive the boundless love of God, knowing that they are valued and cherished by You.

In Jesus' name, we offer this prayer, trusting in Your love and provision.

Amen.

PRAYER FOR THE SINGLES

Dear Heavenly Father,

Today, I bring before You those who are seeking a life partner. Your Word teaches us that a good wife is a gift from You, and I pray for the young men who are on this quest for a life partner. Lord, may they seek You and ask for the perfect gift that You have in store for them.

I pray with confidence that You will grant them the desires of their hearts. We trust in Your promise that every good and perfect gift comes from You, as stated in James 1:17.

Your faithfulness, O Lord, is unwavering, and we thank You in advance for providing them with the beautiful person You have chosen for them.

I lift up a prayer to break every sense of confusion that may cloud their discernment. May Your Spirit grant them the self-control needed as they patiently wait for Your perfect timing. Strengthen their self-control, Lord, so it surpasses the desires of the flesh.

In their search and waiting, I extend my blessings upon them, knowing that Your plans for them are good. In Your name, we offer this prayer, believing in Your providence and guidance.

Amen.

You Don't Need to Worry About This

The LORD did this to me in preparation for the Harvest School (HS22) in Pemba.

I was on the brink of a journey, set to depart the following day. However, the night before my departure, the Lord graced me with a remarkable vision. In this vision, a pastor friend appeared and addressed me, saying, "You are still lacking some essentials for your trip. Fear not, for here they are."

To my astonishment, he presented me with boxes filled with items that I hadn't even considered including in my preparations. These were clearly things I had overlooked. It was a divine revelation, and I took it to heart.

The very next day, as I prepared to embark on my journey, a dear sister in Christ came into the picture. She informed me that she was also headed to Kigali. We decided to navigate the immigration process together. In Rwanda, we faced the task of exchanging currency for bus tickets. Each of us proceeded to handle our own financial transactions.

After securing our bus tickets, my companion expressed her desire to visit the MTN office to obtain a SIM card. I readily accompanied her, and she successfully acquired one.

We proceeded to the bus terminal for ticket payment. As I was about to settle my own fare, she intervened, insisting that she would cover the cost. I initially declined her offer, explaining that I had ample funds for my transportation. However, she remained resolute, insisting that she wanted to take care of this expense as an act of kindness.

During our journey, we engaged in meaningful conversations and shared experiences. At one point, I felt prompted by the Lord to share the vision I had received the previous night. As I narrated the details of the vision, she listened attentively, affirming it as a profound and positive dream.

Curious, she inquired about my connections in Kigali, to which I explained that I typically opted to stay in guesthouses rather than with friends. However, she revealed that she knew of a Korean family's house where she and her husband had frequently lodged during their visits to Kigali. This revelation sparked hope in her eyes.

She recalled, "I've lost their contact number, but I believe my husband may still have it. Let me reach out to him, and perhaps we can arrange to stay at their 'HAPPY HOUSE' guesthouse."

Upon arriving in Kigali, I intended to hire a motorbike to my chosen lodging. Yet, my companion suggested that we take a taxi instead. We embarked on this uncertain journey, navigating the streets without a definite destination. In this moment of uncertainty, she contacted the guesthouse owner, who graciously came to our rescue.

Remarkably, the guesthouse was situated nearby, a mere stone's throw away from where we had wandered. This experience evoked memories of the Israelites' wanderings and the Lord's admonition to them, *"You have circled this mountain long enough"* (Deuteronomy 2:3).

As the day grew late, hunger beckoned, prompting us to visit the Ethiopian restaurant LALIBELA. We enjoyed a delightful meal, and once again, my companion generously covered the expenses.

Subsequently, we set out to return to the guesthouse, but our path led us astray. For nearly an hour and a half, we meandered around before, by God's grace, finding our way back. Once more, my companion paid for the motorbike ride.

The following morning, it was time for me to make my way to the airport. My faithful companion offered a heartfelt prayer for my journey. To ensure a smooth departure, she arranged for a diplomatic vehicle to transport me to the airport.

As we arrived at the airport, she instructed the driver to take me to the checkpoint, handed me a book, and shared, "Please do not lose what's inside."

Perplexed, I opened the book to discover a sum of $30. Her kindness knew no bounds. She remained at the gate until I passed through the security checkpoint. Her willingness to be a vessel of God's provision had eased my travels in remarkable ways.

Reflecting on this entire journey, I came to understand that it was the Lord's divine orchestration. He knew my needs and had provided for them in ways that I couldn't have foreseen. This experience resonated with the wisdom of 1 Corinthians, *"God is faithful, by whom ye were called unto the fellowship of his Son Jesus Christ our Lord"* (1 Corinthians 1:9).

It's a powerful reminder that we don't always comprehend the meaning of visions and dreams the Lord grants us. Often, we doubt or dismiss them. Yet, these visions and dreams serve as channels through which God communicates His intentions to humanity. Job 33:14-15 reinforces this truth: *"For God speaketh once, yea twice, yet man perceiveth it not. In a dream, in a vision of the night, when deep sleep falleth upon men, in slumberings upon the bed."*

In our journeys through life, we need not fret about understanding every step. God knows the way and provides us with His guidance. There is no need for panic or stress when we walk hand in hand with Him on the waters of uncertainty. As we step into each new phase, we can trust that He already knows our tomorrow, the next five years, and the state of our future bank accounts.

Thank you, Lord, for your unwavering knowledge of our destinies and your constant provision. Our hearts are filled with gratitude and praise.

PRAYER FOR OUR FARMERS

"Bread grain is crushed fine, indeed, the farmer does not continue to thresh it forever. Because the wheel of his cart and his horses eventually damage it, He does not thresh it longer." (Isaiah 28:28)

"While the earth remains, Seedtime and harvest, Cold and heat, Winter and summer, and day and night Shall not cease." (Genesis 8:22)

Heavenly Father,

As we enter this new day, we are reminded that it is a day You have crafted and gifted to us. We choose to rejoice and be glad in it, just as Your Word in Psalm 118:24 encourages us.

Dear God, You are not only our Father, but also our Shepherd and Protector. We ask for Your abiding presence throughout the day, not just in our lives but also in the lives of our families as they go about their endeavors. Bless our fields, our crops, and our animals, Lord. May Your favor be upon all we do.

We earnestly pray that Your joy may fill our hearts continuously, and that Your boundless love may permeate our lives in the name of Jesus. May Your light shine within us, guiding our paths towards You, O Lord, for we love You as You first loved us.

With open hearts, we invite You to come and reign as our Lord and Savior. Forgive our sins and our shortcomings, for we belong to You, Lord.

Now, we take a moment to lift up in prayer three to five farmers, expecting Your touch to bless their lives as well. Thank You, Lord, for this beautiful day; we will rejoice and be glad in it.

In the name of Jesus, we pray.

Amen.

PRAYER FOR POSTMEN AND DELIVERY SERVICES

In all labour there is profit, But mere talk leads only to poverty. (Proverbs 14: 23)

Heavenly Father,

We come before You today with gratitude in our hearts for the dedicated men and women who tirelessly deliver letters, packages, food, and flowers to our homes. Despite the challenges of weather and traffic, they faithfully perform their duties, and we thank You for their unwavering dedication.

Lord, on this day, we lift up prayers for their protection as they navigate the bustling traffic. We ask for an outpouring of physical, emotional, and spiritual strength upon them. May Your blessings abound in their lives, and may Your light penetrate their hearts, filling them with Your love and joy.

In the mighty name of Jesus, we declare that every spiritual burden weighing on their shoulders falls away. We rebuke every spirit of addiction and drug abuse, and we command them to leave in the name of Jesus. Let all forms of depression be banished from their lives, never to return.

We pray that Your Holy Spirit envelops them at this very moment, providing comfort and strength. Thank You, Lord, for Your divine protection.

To those who have not yet received Jesus Christ as their Savior and Lord, we extend an invitation to open their hearts to Him. May they recognize that He loves them and is knocking at the door of their hearts, ready to enter.

Now, as children of God, we take a moment to pray for our colleagues and friends who work alongside us. We speak blessings over them in Jesus' name.

Amen.

Let's incorporate Isaiah 40:29 into our prayer: *"Lord, just as Isaiah 40:29 reminds us, we come before You, knowing that You give strength to the weary and increase power to those who have none."*

Shar Healing Over the Phone

Shar, a sister of someone I crossed paths with a decade ago, experienced a profound transformation brought about by the Lord. However, Shar fell critically ill and was scheduled for surgery in a hospital located in a different country. To provide context, we were in Uganda, while Shar was in another nation altogether. Shar's sister urgently contacted me, pleading for prayer on her sister's behalf before she underwent surgery.

In response, I fervently prayed. During our phone conversation, a gentle whisper from the Holy Spirit guided me to instruct Shar to fetch a cup of water and fill a basin. I followed the divine instructions faithfully and humbly relayed them to her.

Shar complied without hesitation, immersing her finger in the cup and then drinking and bathing with the water from the basin. With the prayer concluded, we entrusted her situation to the Lord.

The following day, Shar arrived at the hospital, where she was scheduled for a pre-operative examination. Astonishingly, the doctors reported that they could find no trace of the illness. Consequently, the scheduled operation was cancelled.

Shar's sister called me the next day, joyfully testifying that the operation had been called off because her sister was no longer afflicted by the disease. To provide some background, Shar had been suffering from a perplexing ailment characterized by persistent vomiting, during which foreign objects such as needles, razors, and even blood would inexplicably appear. None of us had been able to discern the nature of this mysterious affliction, and it had severely impacted her health for an extended period.

It was only through fervent prayer that Shar's miraculous deliverance, and healing occurred. Today, she enjoys robust health and vitality, and all the credit for her remarkable recovery goes to Jesus, the miracle worker.

Indeed, Jesus continues to perform wonders, and His divine works know no bounds. The healing bestowed upon Shar serves as a testimony to His boundless power. Regardless of the perplexity or severity of any disease, remember that Jesus can bring about healing and restoration.

As we reflect on this extraordinary testimony, let us remain confident that Jesus is actively working in our lives as well, ready to manifest His miraculous power.

DAY 21

PRAYER FOR MY PARTNER

"And let the [gracious] favor of the Lord our God be on us; Confirm for us the work of our hands—Yes, confirm the work of our hands". (Psalm 90: 17)

"Delight yourself in the Lord, And He will give you the desires and petitions of your heart." (Psalms 37:4)

Heavenly Father,

As the morning light breaks, I humbly bring my beloved partner before Your presence, seeking Your divine protection over their heart, mind, and body throughout the day.

I pray for Your peace to envelop them like a warm embrace and for the joy that springs from knowing You to be their unwavering strength.

May Your radiant light shine upon them wherever they journey today, Lord, making them a beacon of Your love and grace to all they encounter.

I ask that You guide their words and actions, enabling them to be a source of blessings to every person they meet, just as Your Word illuminates their path, as stated in Psalm 119:105.

Lord, I pray that their life may be marked by an abundance of fruitfulness in serving You and others.

In the powerful name of Jesus, I lift up a heartfelt prayer for success, not only in their work but also in their home and in every endeavor they pursue.

May Your favor and blessings flow abundantly in their life today and every day, as we offer this prayer with faith and trust in Your loving guidance.

Amen.

I pray that as they find their delight in You, Lord, You will fulfill the desires of their heart, in accordance with Your Word.

Personal Prayer Guide

Use this page for your personal prayers and impressions. You can use this to write the names of people you are praying for and record testimonies of what God is doing through prayer.

CHAPTER 7

FOUR PRINCIPLES THAT WILL CHANGE YOUR LIFE FOREVER

Let's delve into a profound message rooted in the wisdom of Proverbs 11:24-26. It's a question that often surfaces: Can a Christian attain wealth? The unequivocal answer is 'yes.'

Now, you might wonder, how is such wealth achievable? The Bible offers a treasury of invaluable principles that, when faithfully applied, have transformed countless lives across the globe, leading them to prosperity and affluence. Today, we'll navigate through four potent principles drawn from the word of God, with the intent of integrating them into our own lives.

Proverbs 11:24-26 (NIV) sets the stage for our exploration:

"One person gives freely, yet gains even more; another withholds unduly, but comes to poverty. A generous person will prosper; whoever refreshes others will be refreshed. People curse the one who hoards grain, but they pray God's blessing on the one who is willing to sell."

Join me as we unearth these principles and learn how to apply them to our lives.

1. Giving Freely

Generosity, my friends, is a virtue that challenges the very core of our human nature. Why, you ask? Because parting with something we hold dear tugs at our heartstrings. It's the act of relinquishing, of offering something we cherish to others. In essence, giving embodies love, and it's a practice deeply rooted in the heart of God. Remember the profound words from the book of John 3:16: *"For God so loved the world, that he gave his only Son..."*

True love, my dear friends, is inherently giving. Love and giving are inseparable. Moreover, the act of giving is a liberating experience. It's like setting a captive heart free. And here's the remarkable part: giving doesn't deplete us; instead, it multiplies our blessings. As Proverbs 11:24 wisely states, *"One person gives freely, yet gains even more..."*

As Christians, we carry within us the essence of love, for Christ Himself resides in our hearts. Therefore, it follows that we should be givers. Now, the pivotal question to ponder is this: Do we desire growth, abundance, and increase in our lives?

The resounding answer is a hearty "Yes!" If we earnestly seek this increase, then let's embrace the principle of giving as a cornerstone of our lives. You'll be astonished at how remarkably it leads to abundance. Conversely, holding back and withholding blessings only perpetuates a cycle of need and want.

Let's heed the call to be generous, not just with our material possessions, but with our love, kindness, and compassion. The world yearns for more givers, more lovers, and more generous hearts. Are you ready to step into this transformative journey of giving? I believe you are. And together, we'll witness the extraordinary power of generosity.

2. The Liberal Soul Shall Be Made Fat

In the Old Testament, the term "soul" refers to an individual—a person, regardless of age, gender, or ethnicity. When any of us, young or old, man or woman, from any background, choose to be generous in our giving, we set a remarkable process in motion. In essence, we become enriched, not just materially, but in every aspect of our lives. It's as if an unseen, divine hand stretches out to expand our horizons.

Consider the wisdom found in Proverbs 11:25, which reminds us, *"Whoever brings blessing will be enriched, and one who waters will himself be watered."* This verse underscores the beautiful reciprocity of giving. As we pour blessings into the lives of others, we, in turn, receive blessings in abundance.

Furthermore, let us not forget the profound truth articulated in Proverbs 19:17: *"Whoever is generous to the poor lends to the Lord, and he will repay him for his deed."* When we extend our hearts and resources to those in need, we enter into a divine partnership with God Himself. It's as if we place God in our debt—a debt He joyfully and abundantly repays.

So, my friends, let's embrace the art of giving with open hearts. Let's remember that when we give, we don't just part with material wealth; we unlock the doors to a richer, more meaningful life. In giving, we tap into the limitless abundance of God's blessings.

3. Helping

Assistance is a potent force, often concealed from the eyes of many. Little do they realize that, regardless of social status or circumstances, when we sow seeds of goodness, the Lord has a way of ensuring those seeds are returned to us in due time. Allow me to share a personal story from my childhood, a testament to the power of helping others.

The year was 1990 when a stranger began visiting our family home. He emerged from the depths of the bush, a place far removed from the city, where he had no family or connections. With nowhere else to turn, he sought shelter with us. It was customary for my parents to extend their hospitality, and so our home became his sanctuary. What started as a simple act of kindness soon transformed into a profound bond, and he became an integral part of our family.

However, in 1996, turmoil descended upon the Democratic Republic of Congo as conflict engulfed the nation. Recruitment drives for various army and militia groups swept across the land. I, too, answered the call, enlisting in the regular army under the banner of the AFDL (Alliance of Democratic Forces for Liberation and Democracy). My younger brother, meanwhile, ventured into the militia known as the Mai Mai, a faction situated far from our home. My return in 1997 marked the beginning of a long period of uncertainty regarding my brother's fate.

Three years elapsed, and we received word that my brother had ventured into the dense jungle with a group of boys but had become lost without a way back. Amidst the heartache and worry, hope suddenly rekindled. While patrolling deep within the jungle, my brother heard a familiar voice call out his name—Claude. Turning to locate the source of the voice, he spotted a man signaling him.

Their encounter carried a cryptic message: "Let us meet here tomorrow at the same time." The next day, my brother tried to break free from his unit, yearning for escape. Unfortunately, his companions thwarted his attempt. Determined, he made another effort the following day, successfully reuniting with the mysterious caller.

This enigmatic figure revealed the truth: he knew my brother, even though my brother had no recollection of him. He recounted how our parents had welcomed him into our home when he was a stranger. Touched by our family's kindness, he offered to lead my brother back to his family.

With a twenty-five-liter jerrycan of cooking oil upon his head, my brother embarked on a long and arduous journey through the heart of the rainforest. During this time, anyone who had joined the army was considered a deserter if they fled, so they had to remain hidden. When my brother finally returned home, it was a moment of profound joy. However, due to the risks associated with his past association, we chose to send him far from our city.

Today, I share this remarkable story with you to emphasize the reciprocal nature of assistance. When we extend a helping hand, we may find ourselves in times of need, and it is then that the benevolence we once sowed returns to uplift us. Truly, helping others is an opportunity granted by God, an opportunity where we, too, may find ourselves receiving the help we require.

4. Sell your corn

Selling, in the realm of business, is more than just a transaction; it signifies the art of trade, where one offers their skills or merchandise and reaps rewards in return. Business, as a whole, presents us with opportunities to enhance our financial well-being and secure our livelihoods. Within the world of business, there exist diverse avenues, such as engaging in productive labor or trading commodities.

The wisdom found in the Proverbs reminds us that a diligent individual's mind is perpetually brimming with ideas and ventures that lead to abundance. It encourages us to remain industrious and continuously seek opportunities to contribute our talents and efforts. This ceaseless quest for meaningful occupation is the cornerstone of financial prosperity.

In the grand tapestry of life, selling emerges as one of the most effective means through which the Lord can bless us with abundance. It transcends mere material transactions and extends to the exchange of knowledge and services, offering legitimate avenues to amass wealth.

Let us delve into the Scriptures to uncover further insights on the principles of diligence and the rewards of industriousness. In Proverbs 12:24, we find guidance: *"The hand of the dili-*

gent will rule, while the slothful will be put to forced labor." This verse underscores the importance of diligence, as it not only leads to prosperity, but also positions one for leadership and authority.

Furthermore, the book of Ecclesiastes, in chapter 9, verse 10, emphasizes the significance of wholehearted dedication to one's endeavors: "Whatever your hand finds to do, do it with your might, for there is no work or thought or knowledge or wisdom in Sheol, to which you are going."

Selling, therefore, is not merely a means of financial gain, but a manifestation of our God-given potential to create, contribute, and thrive. Whether we offer tangible goods or intangible services, our commitment to diligent work and principled trade can lead to increased prosperity, and a life filled with purpose. So, let us embrace the opportunities before us, selling not only products but also our skills, talents, and knowledge, as we journey toward the fulfillment of God's blessings and our own financial well-being.

CHAPTER 8

PRAYERS FOR LIVING ACCORDING TO GOD'S WILL

The Chini Story

It all began on a significant day, July 21, 2015, a day etched in my memory.

That morning, as the sun heralded a new day, we gathered for class at 8 a.m. following our worship session. Rolland Baker, the instructor, embarked on a profound exploration of the kingdom of God, delivering his teachings with intricate depth. I was profoundly moved and enriched by his insights, finding great blessings in his words.

After another session of worship and praise, Heidi Baker took the stage to impart her teachings on the Beatitudes. Her words resonated deeply within us, painting a vivid picture of God's blessings upon the humble and meek. As the clock neared 1:15 p.m., she prepared to conclude her teaching but not without igniting a fervent hunger for Jesus within our hearts. I distinctly recall her impassioned query, "Who desires more of Jesus?"

In that moment, I knelt in earnest, arms raised in desperate surrender. My head bowed, and an overwhelming presence enveloped me. The atmosphere was charged with an unusual power, and I remained in a state of profound awe.

Suddenly, Heidi beckoned us to join hands for a prayer of impartation. I couldn't open my eyes, ensnared by the divine energy that coursed through me. It was Heidi herself who laid hands on me, offering fervent supplication. I found myself on the ground, rolling under the influence of this potent impartation. Even as I recount this experience, the memory of that overwhelming power lingers with me.

Afterward, Heidi embraced me, and with an amplified infusion of the Holy Spirit, I rose and embraced her in return. Her fiery spirit was palpable, leaving an indelible mark on my soul. Inexplicably, I burst into uncontrollable laughter that persisted until I reached the cafeteria, where exhaustion overcame me, and I drifted into slumber.

In that moment of rest, I was transported into a vision. I found myself in the presence of Papa Rolland Baker, who conveyed a specific message. He spoke of a pastor in need, yet the details of this person's location and identity remained shrouded in mystery.

Upon waking, I visited the bathroom briefly before returning to bed, where another vision awaited. This time, Papa Rolland stood alongside two young girls who had come for impartation. It was a remarkable sight as he touched these children, and they were instantly overwhelmed by the Spirit of God, erupting into joyous laughter.

In the same night, the Lord granted me yet another vision. Papa Rolland was seated, and my attention was drawn to an elderly man draped in a traditional Kaplana fabric. A second individual approached and, with great simplicity, requested a cup of tea from the man wearing the Kaplana.

The elderly man then beckoned me closer, proclaiming, "Roland, you are a mighty man of God. The best days of your life lie ahead, and you shall be blessed." A moment later, he humbly apologized, uttering, "Mea culpa."

In this vision, Papa Rolland patiently corrected the man's actions, demonstrating grace and understanding. Witnessing this exchange, I perceived that the man was reluctant to return home until he had been cleansed of his shame. The voice of the vision emphasized, "NEVER FORGET THIS. This is your calling."

As I prepared to depart from this transcendent place, Rolland Baker summoned me and disclosed, "The pastor in need requires someone who can communicate in both English and Chini."

I hesitated, inquiring, "Is this Chini a form of Chinese?"

He clarified, "No, it's not precisely Chinese, but it bears similarities. It's akin to a dialect."

Though initially unfamiliar with Chini, I soon yielded to divine purpose, declaring, "God, I am here. Send me. I am willing to learn and serve the community."

In the absence of a mobile phone or computer to research, a fellow student I met at our school 22 took it upon herself to search for information on my behalf, faithfully assisting in uncovering the vision I received.

The way the Lord orchestrated events like this left me utterly amazed and reinforced my unwavering belief that God has an intimate knowledge of every person on Earth, regardless of their background or location. It serves as undeniable evidence that God not only created each individual but also deeply loves and cares for them. In that moment, I realized that He was seeking someone to respond with, "Here I am, Lord. Send me."

PRAYER FOR IMMIGRATION OFFICERS

"And [pray] that we will be rescued from perverse and evil men; for not everyone has the faith." (2 Thessalonians 3:2)

Heavenly Father,

As I embark on this new day, whether leaving my home for work or already seated at my office desk, I pause to pray with a heart open to You. Here I am, surrendering my day, my workplace, my thoughts, my heart, and my entire life into Your loving hands. May Your presence reign in every aspect of my life.

I pray that You infuse me with an abundance of joy and love as I handle the various tasks and paperwork that come my way. Lord, extend Your protective shield around me, and may Your blessings overflow upon my family as they remain at home. I entrust my journeys, both to and from work, into Your guiding hands. Thank You, Jesus.

Now, I beseech You to grant me the strength and courage to stand firmly for justice, resisting any temptations or solicitations that suggest corruption or injustice.

In Jesus' mighty name, I declare the breaking of every form of addiction and the dispelling of lies that may have entangled my life. I ask for Your forgiveness for all my mistakes and sins, and I open the door of my heart for You to enter as my Lord and Savior. Amen.

Lord, I also take a moment to lift up in prayer the immigration officers. May Your ministering presence touch their lives and guide them in their duties. We thank You, Lord, for Your unfailing love and grace. Amen.

The voice in the night

After a dedicated ten days of fasting and prayer, the Lord spoke to me with a divine mission: "I will send you to my people, and you will speak to them about me." This divine calling led me to a foreign country I had never imagined visiting before. Guided by God's providence, I managed to secure a humble single room as my dwelling place.

In the adjacent room resided a devout Christian family, wholeheartedly devoted to serving Jesus. Their warm hospitality and boundless generosity radiated the love of Christ. They were actively engaged in their local church, a testament to their unwavering faith.

One ordinary day, as I immersed myself in the Scriptures, contemplating the profound Word of God, there came a gentle knock on my door. I promptly answered, and to my surprise, it was my neighbor, Mr. OB, paying me a visit. As is customary in this land, I offered him a soda as a sign of hospitality and respect.

With a kind and concerned demeanor, Mr. OB inquired about my well-being. I assured him that I was doing well, though puzzled by the reason for his visit. What followed was a message that left me in awe.

"You know," Mr. OB began, "I've been observing you during your stay here. The Lord spoke to my wife and me, instructing us to take care of your food needs. Therefore, please do not concern yourself with what you will eat or drink."

His words resonated with divine guidance, and it felt as though he was reciting verses from the Bible. Overwhelmed with gratitude, I couldn't help but ask if there were any expectations on my part.

Mr. OB quickly dismissed such thoughts, shaking his head with a warm smile. "No, no," he reassured me. "It is God who sent you here, and He has entrusted us with the task of providing for you."

Brothers and sisters, I want to confess that even though God had miraculously provided for my rent, I still grappled with uncertainty regarding food. However, Mr. OB's visit served as a reminder of God's unwavering care and His provision through unexpected angels. On my knees, I offered heartfelt thanks to God for the divine messenger He had sent into my life.

The first year had been a season of blessings and abundance, marked by God's provision and Mr. OB's unwavering generosity. As the second year commenced, it began on a promising note, with life continuing its harmonious course. However, as time passed, an unexpected turn of events disrupted the rhythm of my daily sustenance.

Gradually, I found myself unable to procure food, and a cloud of uncertainty veiled the reason behind this sudden change. Yet, I hesitated to inquire, fearing that perhaps Mr. OB's goodwill had ceased or some unseen circumstance had arisen. Life assumed a semblance of normalcy once more, and I chose to maintain my silence. Gratitude remained my constant companion as I reflected on the period when sustenance had flowed freely, and I thanked God for the family's exceptional generosity.

One evening, after returning from the evening prayer and settling into my room, I found myself enveloped in a moment of solitude. Expressing my gratitude to the Almighty for the day's blessings, I was jolted by a sudden knock on my door. I swiftly responded to the summons, ushering Mr. OB into my humble abode. Although the confines of my dwelling did not boast chairs, I offered him a seat on the floor—a practical choice in this land where space was a cherished commodity.

With a warm exchange of pleasantries, I inquired about his well-being, my curiosity piqued by his somewhat hesitant demeanor. Sensing a weighty matter on his mind, I encouraged him to share his concerns.

"Uhhh, err..." Mr. OB began, his words laden with uncertainty.

I leaned forward attentively. "What is it?" I inquired.

He shook his head, grappling with the words. "No, you must forgive me," he implored, his eyes reflecting a sense of guilt.

Perplexed, I responded, "Why should I forgive you? You've committed no offense against me."

Mr. OB's urgency intensified as he sought to convey the gravity of his revelation. "No, no, you do not understand," he insisted.

Puzzled, I pressed further, "What is it that I do not comprehend?"

With a sigh, he decided to confide in me. "Allow me to explain," he began. "You may have noticed that we stopped providing you with food. It was a decision my wife and I made in secret. However, since we ceased, an inexplicable phenomenon unfolded. Our food supply plummeted drastically, and we found ourselves on the brink of depletion."

His voice tinged with remorse, he continued, "Moreover, just last night, I had a vivid dream—a dream where a man rebuked me sternly. He questioned why we had halted the provision of food to 'his son' and emphasized the gravity of this decision. He asked if we were aware of the source of our sustenance."

Pausing briefly, he locked eyes with me and confessed, "In a strange twist, my wife had experienced the same dream, wherein she, too, was reprimanded for concurring with the decision to cease supplying you with food. Therefore, I have come here today, burdened by our ill-fated choice, to apologize on behalf of my family. We acknowledge our error, and we intend to reinstate our support. Will you kindly accept food from us once more?"

Without hesitation, I offered my forgiveness and acceptance. "Yes, of course. I hold no grudge, and I forgive you," I reassured him.

With a shared prayer for reconciliation and renewed goodwill, Mr. OB departed, leaving behind a sense of restoration and a testament to the transformative power of forgiveness.

The profound truth we must grasp is that nothing we undertake, whether it occurs in the shadows or under the glaring light of day, remains concealed from the omniscient gaze of our Creator. This understanding aligns perfectly with the words of Psalm 139:11-12, which declare, *"If I say, 'Surely the darkness will hide me, and the light become night around me,' even the darkness is not dark to You, but the night shines like the day, for darkness is as light to You."*

We are compelled to ponder the age-old question posed in Psalms 8:4, *"What is man that You are mindful of him, and the son of earthborn man that You care for him?"* This query, rooted in humility, resounds with deep significance in this narrative.

Yet, amidst our reflections, let us bestow commendation upon this individual for his swift response to the divine call. How often do we, in our frailty, wrestle with the obedience that God's voice demands? We ought to applaud him not only for his humility but also for the tender contrition of his heart. His example serves as a powerful reminder that we should not await the depletion of our resources before we heed the Lord's directives.

Indeed, as articulated in Luke 12:48, *"From everyone to whom much has been given, much will be required; and to whom they entrusted much, of him they will ask all the more."* This principle underscores the significance of our faithful stewardship, even when our supply abounds, as a testament to our unwavering commitment to God's call.

What is God asking of you right now? Take some time and reflect on this question.

PRAYER FOR MY CHILDREN

Heavenly Father,

As I embrace this new morning, my heart swells with gratitude for the precious gifts You've bestowed upon me — my beloved children, [Name each one of them]. Each of them is a cherished blessing from Your loving hands.

I pray that Your divine protection encircles them like a fortress as they embark on their daily journeys, whether it be to work, school, or the playground. Lord, I entrust their safety to You, asking that no harm shall befall them.

Thank You, Lord, for crafting them in a wondrous and unique manner. I pray that they may personally encounter Your loving presence, developing a deep and abiding relationship with You.

May Your abundant blessings accompany them throughout their lives, and may they, in turn, become beacons of Your blessings to anyone they encounter.

Lord, I implore You to utilize their lives as instruments of Your divine purpose, guiding them in different spheres of life, and guarding them against the allure of negative influences that may lead them astray.

Heavenly Father, I ask that You bless their dreams and aspirations, and may they come to know You intimately, sharing Your love with others.

Grant them the grace of parenthood when the time is right, and endow them with the wisdom to nurture and guide their own children.

I beseech You, Holy Spirit, to be their constant guide in making wise and responsible life choices. Instill in them the wisdom to manage their finances and careers in a manner that honors You, regardless of their societal positions.

With heartfelt praise, I thank You, Lord, for the incredible gift of each one of my children and grandchildren.

In Jesus' name, I offer this prayer, trusting in Your boundless love and grace.

Amen.

Just like David praying over Salomon, I pray: *"And give unto Solomon my son, a perfect heart, to keep thy commandments, thy testimonies, and thy statutes, and to do all these things, and to build the palace, for the which I have made provision."*
1 Chronicles 29:19

Personal Prayer Guide

Use this page for your personal prayers and impressions. You can use this to write the names of people you are praying for and record testimonies of what God is doing through prayer.

CHAPTER 9

PRAYERS FOR GOD'S WONDERS

The Mysterious Fire

It was the cusp of July, and the anticipation for our Friday night prayers had swelled within the hearts of our congregation. The fervor was palpable as we had all unanimously agreed to gather in unity for this sacred event. As the appointed hour approached, I made my way to the church, eager to partake in this spiritual communion. To my surprise, I was the first to arrive.

Soon, a lady entered, followed by two others who joined us in our vigil. We waited in hopeful expectation, yearning for more of our brethren to join our assembly. However, as minutes turned into moments and time marched on, it became apparent that we would be a small, intimate group for this special night of prayer.

Unfazed by the modest turnout, I discerned that we should commence our prayers without delay. It is essential to note that our humble church edifice nestled adjacent to a brothel, a place rife with iniquity and debauchery that perpetually surrounded us. On this particular night, the sordid activities of the brothel escalated, their cacophonous wails and pungent odors infiltrating our sacred space through the thin plastic walls. We stood resolute in the face of this spiritual battleground, acutely aware of the looming battle.

Undeterred by the ominous atmosphere, we began to pray fervently. However, as the spiritual battle intensified, we found ourselves gradually succumbing to weariness. One by one, my fellow warriors succumbed to fatigue, and I was left grappling with a profound sense of uncertainty, unsure of how to navigate this spiritual crossroads.

Suddenly, a righteous indignation surged within me, and I roused my slumbering companions. "You, take your place there, and you, stand here, and you, right there," I directed, positioning each of them in strategic places. "I shall stand behind you all."

Our outstretched arms pointed towards the sinister silhouette of the brothel that loomed ominously nearby. With resolute determination, I declared, "Together, let us exert our collective strength to expel this malevolent presence from our midst." In a mere three minutes that felt both fleeting and eternal, we strained with all our might, but soon found ourselves drained of words and energy, collapsing in exhaustion.

Then, as if guided by divine providence, a profound slumber enveloped us, transporting us into the realm of dreams.

When we awoke, it was Saturday morning. Gently, I turned to my fellow prayer warriors, saying, "Let us return home and attempt to recover from the shock of last night's spiritual battle." It was our custom to hold intercessory prayers every Saturday morning from 9:00 a.m. to 12:00 p.m., yet on this occasion, it appeared that none had gathered.

However, unbeknownst to us, God had spoken to Mr. Kan on that fateful Friday night, urging him to spend the night at the church. Consequently, on Saturday, he dutifully made his way to the church and remained there throughout the night. In the midst of those dark hours, he bore witness to a miraculous sight—an ethereal fire, manifesting from the unseen, descended upon the brothel. With remarkable foresight, he saved several precious items from the church premises.

Upon our return the following morning, an astonishing and devastating sight greeted us. The entire vicinity had been reduced to smoldering ashes. The landowner, curious and compassionate, arrived with a group of concerned individuals to ascertain the cause of the calamity. In awe of the divine intervention, she proclaimed, "A true God exists. I have long yearned for these occupants to vacate, but I could not bring myself to ask them to leave."

Then, with a gracious gesture, she turned to us and declared, "You are free to build your church upon this entire parcel of land."

Witness the undeniable efficacy of prayer—its power to transform circumstances, align destinies, and evoke divine intervention. Indeed, God is capable of using His divine authority with profound impact, even with the utterance of a brief, earnest prayer. The consequences reverberate, reshaping not only the physical landscape but the spiritual destinies of those it touches.

In the wake of this awe-inspiring event, the young man who once owned the accursed brothel experienced a profound conversion, turning away from his past life of sin to embrace the gospel he had once persecuted. He walked the path of redemption and reconciliation, ultimately finding peace in the loving arms of the Lord.

DAY 24

PRAYER FOR OUR PILOTS

"But those who wait for the Lord [who expect, look for, and hope in Him] Will gain new strength and renew their power; They will lift up their wings [and rise up close to God] like eagles [rising toward the sun]; They will run and not become weary. They will walk and not grow tired."
Isaiah 40:31

Heavenly Father,

As pilots embark on their journeys today, I lift them up in prayer, acknowledging Your sovereignty over their flights. I beseech You to guide their every movement, ensuring safe travel for all.

I pray, Lord, for the personal protection of these pilots, as well as for the well-being of their dedicated cabin crews and the precious passengers entrusted to their care. May the boundless love of God fill their hearts as they navigate the skies and safely bring their aircraft to its destination.

Grant them, O Lord, the gift of wisdom to make sound decisions throughout their daily tasks. I also bring before You the families they have temporarily left behind. May Your divine protection and blessings encompass their loved ones, and may the radiance of Your face shine brightly upon them.

Lord Jesus, we unite in prayer, acknowledging Your superior

leadership. We implore You to take the helm of their journeys today. We open our hearts to welcome You as our King, Lord, and Savior. Forgive us for our countless sins and mistakes, and make Your divine presence known within us. May Your light continuously illuminate our hearts.

I extend my prayers to include my colleagues in this endeavor, [Name them], and every soul on board. Thank You, Lord, for Your boundless grace and protection.

In Your holy name, we pray.

Amen

Tomorrow you will be arrested

It was a joyous Sunday afternoon, filled with songs of praise and worship that resonated throughout the gathering. The people were united in their celebration, offering heartfelt thanks to the living God for their new place of worship. Gone were the days when they were relegated to a cramped corner, and the joyous shouts of church members echoed with gratitude.

As the celebration drew to a close, it was time to conclude the festivities, clean up, and return all the items used for the grand opening of their new church location. With a friend by my side, each of us carried a crate filled with empty soda bottles, one on the left and the other on the right. We engaged in a conversation about the remarkable events of the day and the distinctive atmosphere of the service.

"Did you notice how we gathered on that expansive concrete floor?" my friend inquired. "The spaciousness of this new place is truly a testament to the goodness of the Lord," he continued, his voice filled with gratitude.

Our journey led us back to our old location, where we had to leave behind our equipment. This space served as a church in the morning, transformed into someone's home during the daytime, and reverted to a place of worship in the evening, only to become someone's residence once more at night.

Before parting ways, my friend reminded me of our choir practice scheduled for the next day. "I'll see you at choir practice," he said, his back turned towards me. "Don't forget, we have a home visit planned for tonight as well. See you then."

Exhausted from the extensive preparations for the ceremony, I found comfort on the couch and gradually drifted into a deep, restorative slumber.

In a vivid vision, I witnessed a scene where an incalculable number of police officers surrounded a highly esteemed man of God. They apprehended him, and it seemed as though his feet didn't even touch the ground – it was as if he had wings. The police officers swarmed around him, and I watched as they forcibly threw this prestigious man of God into prison.

Time seemed to stretch on, and eventually, he was released from prison. However, he fled the city where he had once lived. In the same vision, I saw that it was the very first day in his new location, and a man directed us back to the former place of worship. It was revealed to me that the church service had begun as usual, but after the prominent leader's arrest, the congregation scattered in fear for their lives. Some returned, while others never did.

Suddenly, I woke up from this unsettling vision, filled with terror at what I had just witnessed. A knock at my door startled me, and to my astonishment, it was the same man from my vision. He found me visibly distressed and fearful.

Sitting down, he inquired, "How did today's service go?"

Overwhelmed and unable to respond immediately, I remained silent.

Growing concerned, he shook me gently and asked, "Are you alright?"

With hesitation, I replied, "No, I am not."

"What's troubling you? I know you well! Did you receive a revelation?" he inquired.

Tears welled up in my eyes as I spoke with trembling words, "Tomorrow, you will be arrested, and today was the last day in that building. Everyone is going to scatter in fear."

"Timothy, Timothy," he said, tapping my shoulder. "Stay strong and wait for the Lord," he encouraged me.

As Monday morning arrived, our regular morning devotional gathered at 5:45 AM, but it was unlike any other day. The news of the prominent man of God's arrest dominated our discussions. Strangely, the church premises were devoid of people – everyone had fled, and others were hesitant to show up. It was as if everything had transpired in the blink of an eye.

Several years later, without any prior communication, he found me on Facebook and shared a message.

FEB 20, 2020, 6:39 PM

Unaweza kumbuka ndoto zenyi ulikuwaka unaniloteyaka kama dunia ?yote itajuwaka msg yangu

FEB 21, 2020, 654 AM

Ndiyo

Mungu ni mwema sana

FEB 21, 2020, 7:40 AM

Nikikumbuka ndoto zako kwangu kisha nikaanguka. île maono haingetimilikiaka mumaono ya mtu mwengine

Translation: Do you remember the visions you had about me?

The second line reads: When I remember your dreams and visions for me. Then I fell short. I know those visions could have never fitted into somebody else's vision. See, God works out miracles!

PRAYER FOR WRITERS AND AUTHORS

"Thus says the Lord God of Israel, 'Write in a book all the words which I have spoken to you". (Jeremiah 30:2)

"And He who sits on the throne said, Behold, I am making all things new.' Also, He said, Write, for these words are faithful and true' [they are accurate, incorruptible, and trustworthy]." (Revelation 21:5)

———

Heavenly Father,

Today, I come before You, lifting up all those individuals who carry within them a treasury of ideas waiting to be transcribed into words that will touch the hearts of many.

Lord, I pray for an outpouring of creativity and inspiration among writers, especially those whom You have divinely inspired to convey the greatness of Your works. May they become eloquent storytellers of Your magnificent deeds.

I pray, dear Lord, for authors who will have the privilege of hearing Your voice directly and faithfully transcribing the truths revealed to them. May their writings be a beacon, illuminating the path back to You for nations far and wide. I pray for those who are uncertain where to begin; may Your Holy Spirit encounter them and set them on their path.

Thank You, Father, for the abundant inspiration You bestow upon writers and authors. We are grateful for the works You will use to transform lives and draw nations closer to You. May Your divine works be recorded and spread throughout the world. We thank You for the vessels You are currently using and those You will raise in the future.

Bless each of these writers and authors, Lord, as they embark on this sacred journey. May their words resonate with truth, grace, and love.

In the name of Jesus, we pray.

Amen.

Personal Prayer Guide

Use this page for your personal prayers and impressions. You can use this to write the names of people you are praying for and record testimonies of what God is doing through prayer.

CHAPTER 10

DEALING WITH ACCUSATION

How to respond to accusations within the church
In our present times, we can observe the presence of malevolent forces at work even within the church. Many church leaders find themselves ensnared in the snares of false accusations, creating turmoil within the congregation.

The Bible, in its wisdom, refers to Satan as "the accuser of the brethren," highlighting the adversary's role in these disruptive events. Indeed, it is evident that he continues to actively influence events within the church.

Before I delve into how we should respond to these internal accusations, allow me to share a recent incident involving a particular church. In its early days, this church burned with a fervent passion for the Lord, and His mighty works were abundantly manifest among the congregation. The tangible presence of God filled their gatherings, leading to a significant expansion of the church community. This growth eventually resulted in the establishment of a sister church.

As the church branched out and acquired new property, the senior pastor made the decision to lead the newly formed congregation on this fresh spiritual journey.

Time passed, and days turned into weeks, months, and eventually years. Throughout this period, the Lord continued to pour out His spiritual and material blessings upon the church. Numerous projects were initiated on the church property, all under the unwavering guidance of the new church pastor, who steadfastly relied on God for His blessings, provision, and divine leadership.

To help clarify the narrative, let's refer to the original church as Church A and the sister church as Church B.

After several years of growth and prosperity, Church A began to experience a shift in dynamics. Internal conflicts arose within the leadership, leading to a significant split within the congregation.

Meanwhile, Church B continued to thrive, firmly under the Lord's divine guidance.

Then, one day, the lead pastor of Church B received a divine message from the Lord. He was told that the new year would bring both challenges and opportunities to support the Lord's work.

Just a few days later, troubling reports reached him, revealing that members of his church were receiving messages from the pastor's wife of Church A. These messages accused him of spreading rumors about the church's split.

In reality, Church B's pastor had not made any such statements or fueled discord in any way.

Faced with this brewing conflict between the two churches, the pastor of Church B found himself at a crossroads. He wondered how best to bring about reconciliation and peace for himself and the people he led.

It is often easy for preachers to quote scripture, declaring that the devil is the accuser of the brethren. However, what happens when this accuser uses a brother or sister within the faith as a vessel for discord?

Accusations from distant individuals may carry less weight, but when they come from close friends and trusted confidants, the emotional impact can be profound, causing deep hurt and distress.

The question remains, how does one respond?

Ways to handle accusations

1. Confront with love

Distinguishing between mere accusations and seeking truth through communication is a crucial aspect of addressing conflicts within the Christian community. It is one thing to hear someone accuse you, but it is another to engage in dialogue with that person. The power of truth always prevails over falsehood, no matter how quickly false information may spread.

In our Christian walk, the Bible provides clear guidance, commanding us not to engage in the spreading of false accusations about our neighbors. This divine directive is rooted in principles of love, integrity, and reconciliation that are central to the teachings of Scripture.

Exodus 23:1: *"You shall not spread a false report. You shall not join hands with a wicked man to be a malicious witness."*

1 Peter 3:16: *"Having a good conscience so that, when you are slandered, those who revile your good behavior in Christ may be put to shame."*

Proverbs 25:8ESV: *"Do not hastily bring into court, for what will you do in the end, when your neighbor puts you to shame?"*

2. Remember your calling

Reflecting on your divine calling becomes especially vital when the adversary employs fellow brothers or sisters to level false accusations against you. Such tactics are intended to divert your attention away from what truly matters, enticing you to fixate on futile matters. In these moments, recalling your God-given calling can help realign your focus and keep you on track. In the following chapter, we will delve deeper into this concept, exploring how it can provide strength and guidance in times of adversity. 1 Peter 3:9 (ESV): *"Do not repay evil for evil or reviling for reviling, but on the contrary, bless, for to this you were called, that you may obtain a blessing."*

3. Accusations are common

Is it not disheartening to witness accusations surfacing within the community of those you hold dear and who, in return, hold you dear? I, too, once believed it unlikely to transpire within the church, but alas, it is an undeniable reality. Accusations are among us. When I say they are common, I draw attention to the pages of Scripture. Consider the plight of Joseph, who endured false accusations. Ponder upon the life of our Lord, Jesus, who faced baseless charges and many more similar instances scattered throughout biblical narratives.

Nehemiah 5:6 (AMP): *"Then I was very angry when I heard their outcry and these words [of accusation]."*

John 18:29: *"So, Pilate came out to them and asked, "What accusation do you bring against this Man?"*

4. Look how blessed you are

The Scriptures offer us a profound insight: you are indeed blessed when false accusations are hurled your way, especially when these accusations are borne out of your allegiance to the Lord's name.

Matthew 5:11 ESV: *"Blessed are you when others revile you and persecute you and utter all kinds of evil against you falsely on my account."*

5. Talk to a friend who understands

Dealing with false accusations can be deeply painful, and during such trying times, it is essential to have a trustworthy friend by your side – someone who is not only physically present but also intimately acquainted with your life. This friend should be capable of speaking the truth into your situation, offering comfort and guidance.

6. Pray

The prayerful state is a position of great power. I often emphasize that prayer isn't about trying to convince the Divine of your perspective, but rather, it's an opportunity for deep communion and fellowship with God.

When you engage in prayer, you are not merely making requests; you are opening your heart to the Lord, sharing your innermost thoughts and feelings. In this sacred space, God imparts His perfect wisdom, offering guidance tailored to your specific needs. Prayer is where you emerge strengthened, emotionally healed, and refocused, for the Lord understands the depths of your heart like no other.

Reflecting on Genesis 50:20 ESV, we find profound wisdom: *"As for you, you meant evil against me, but God meant it for good, to bring it about that many people should be kept alive, as they are today."* This verse reminds us that even in the face of adversity and false accusations, God can turn the situation around for our ultimate good and the benefit of many.

Meanwhile, The Devil Is Feasting On Your Sheep

Let's revisit the narrative of churches A and B, and take a moment to carefully consider these words. It's essential to acknowledge that the devil, known as the accuser of the brethren, inflicts deep wounds when it's a fellow brother or sister in the Lord who falsely accuses you.

It's crucial to understand that when the devil sows seeds of accusation within the church, his intentions are far-reaching and multifaceted. It's not merely about targeting one individual; his scope is more extensive than the isolated instances we often hear about.

I often emphasize that the devil thrives when leaders within the church become entangled in disputes fueled by accusations. But what exactly do I mean by this? In an earlier section, I alluded to the devil's broader objectives behind accusations within the church, and now, let's delve deeper into this matter.

Primarily, the devil has a multi-pronged agenda when it comes to accusations within the church:

1. **Divert Your Focus:** His first goal is to draw your attention away from your divine calling and purpose within the church. Accusations can be a cunning distraction that keeps you preoccupied with defending your reputation rather than serving the Lord wholeheartedly.
2. **Sow Confusion:** The devil seeks to inject confusion and discord into the congregation. When accusations fly, it can fracture the unity of believers, causing strife and division among them.
3. **Bring Shame:** Another sinister objective is to tarnish the reputation of church leaders. By accusing them falsely, the devil aims to shame and discredit those who are in positions of spiritual authority.

These tactics mirror the devil's schemes as described in the Bible. In 2 Corinthians 2:11 (NIV), we are warned not to be ignorant of his schemes: *"in order that Satan might not outwit us. For we are not unaware of his schemes."*

Understanding these tactics equips us to stand firm against the devil's attempts to disrupt the peace and unity of the church.

Furthermore, it is well-established that the enemy's intentions are to steal, kill, and destroy. Meanwhile, the senior pastor of Church B found himself inundated with an increasing number of individuals, far more than before, who were voicing their concerns about the following:

1. Tormenting the Flock

During this troubling period, members of the church began to approach the pastor with their sleepless nights and agonizing torment. One poignant account involved a woman who, in despair, confided, "I can't even close my eyes for fear that the nightmares haunting me will return. I've reached a breaking point, so much so that I've contemplated self-harm." The pastor devoted an entire week to fervent prayer with her, and gradually, the layers of diabolical oppression encasing her life were unveiled. Yet, it's crucial to remember that Jesus came to grant us not only life but life in abundance. Today, she stands as a testimony to God's deliverance, living a life unburdened by fear.

Another heart-wrenching tale involved a pregnant woman ensnared in a web of dark sorcery, manipulated into considering the unthinkable – ending her own child's life. Desperation drove her to seek help from witch doctors, but their efforts proved futile. Only when she turned to the church did the

Lord intervene, freeing both her and her unborn child. Remember, Jesus came to offer us life in abundance.

Do you grasp the dire situation in which the enemy feasts upon the vulnerable sheep while the shepherd's attention is diverted?

2. Creating a Breeding Ground for Sin

During this tumultuous period, sin stealthily infiltrated the congregation. Immoral relationships festered, and promiscuity ran rampant, seemingly unchecked. In the narrative of churches A and B, sin had become the prevailing lifestyle for many. One young woman approached the pastor, burdened by the weight of a hidden and sinful existence, confessing her inner turmoil. Adultery and illicit affairs tore through the community like wildfire. It was as though a voracious spiral had engulfed them all.

In Galatians 5, the Bible warns, *"But if you bite and devour one another [in bickering and strife], watch out that you [along with your entire fellowship] are not consumed by one another."* Observing this, one can't help but question the whereabouts of spiritual discernment and the clarity of the people's vision. However, the truth remains that during this tumultuous period, the devil was feasting upon the vulnerable sheep. It took individuals with the courage of David, who faced the roaring and devouring lion, to break free from this cycle of destruction. It was the intervention of Jesus that shattered the chains of bondage and brought praise to the Lord.

3. Causing spiritual sleepiness

Clearly, when chaos engulfs the church, a sense of mediocrity often permeates. Prayer life dwindles, and the love among members grows cold. Even the hunger for God's Word diminishes.

During this period, service attendance experienced a significant decline, and the atmosphere during prayer and worship became notably heavy. Vulnerability to deception became more prevalent.

CHAPTER 11

PRAYERS
FOR ENDURANCE

Almost separated yet fully restored

Allow me to share a remarkable encounter involving a couple visited by the pastor, which left him utterly astounded.

As the pastor inquired why they had been conspicuously absent from church services, their response struck him like a bolt of lightning.

"We're on the brink of separation," the husband confessed.

The pastor, bewildered, sought clarification. "Separation? What do you mean?"

The husband, with a heavy heart, elaborated, "You've arrived at a crucial juncture; my wife and I are contemplating divorce. Take a glance at her packed bags, and I temporarily withheld her ID while we arrange for the children."

This revelation was a stark reminder that the thief, whose sole purpose is to steal, kill, and destroy, was actively at work. However, Jesus came not only to counteract these destructive forces but to bring restoration to broken lives and relationships.

Miraculously, through the intervention of the pastor and the grace of the Lord, this struggling marriage was not only saved but fully restored!

Let this serve as a testament to the transformative power of faith and the unwavering belief in God's ability to mend the most shattered of bonds.

PRAYER FOR CHURCH LEADERS

"And I will give you shepherds according to My heart, who will feed you with knowledge and understanding".
Jeremiah 3:15

Heavenly Father, today I lift up those whom you have appointed as leaders within the church. I pray that you grant them unwavering courage to continue preaching the message of Jesus Christ, even in the face of opposition. Strengthen them, Lord, so that they may endure and persevere through any hardships that may arise in their homes, lives, communities, and within the church.

Lord, I beseech you to fortify their resolve to stand firm and resist compromise. Instill within them a deep hunger for your Word and a thirst for the Living Water, that they may continually nourish themselves from your divine source.

Grant these church leaders the wisdom, love, and guidance needed to tend to and shepherd the flock you have entrusted to their care. May they be diligent in preparing your bride for the glorious meeting with you, our Lord.

I also pray, Lord, that those among them who require emotional, financial, or spiritual support will receive divine assistance from Heaven. We thank you, Lord, for these dedicated church leaders who serve your people with love and devotion. In Jesus' name, we pray. Amen.

PRAYER FOR MISSIONARIES

Heavenly Father, we come before you with hearts full of gratitude for those you have called to serve as missionaries, both within their own nations and abroad. We acknowledge the great need for disciple-makers in this world, and we earnestly pray for you to send forth more laborers into the harvest fields. Father, may many heed your call and step forward to answer it.

We lift up each missionary to you, Lord, asking for your blessings to abound in their lives. Please provide for all their needs according to your boundless riches. Safeguard their souls, we pray, and protect them from the spiritual numbness that can sometimes befall those on the mission field. Instead, grant them an unquenchable spirit of exploration and a burning desire to continue their mission with passion.

For the missionaries in our own country, we pray that they may always rely on you and witness your provision in their daily lives. Strengthen their resolve to stand firmly for the gospel, and use them as instruments to bring many into your kingdom.

Father, we beseech you to send even more missionaries to our country and raise up those from our nation to go out into the world. Grant them health, strength, and resilience in all aspects of their lives—emotionally, physically, and spiritually.

Lord Jesus, we humbly ask that you transform the mindset of missionaries from one of authority to that of a humble servant.

May they emulate your example as they work tirelessly for your glory. We thank you, Lord, for using these missionaries to further your kingdom and spread your love to the ends of the earth. In Jesus' name, we pray. Amen.

PRAYER FOR THE SENIORS

Heavenly Father, we come before you today with hearts full of reverence and gratitude for our seniors, the golden treasures of our communities. Your Word teaches us in Proverbs 16:31 that *"Gray hair is a crown of glory; it is gained in a righteous life."* We thank you for the wisdom, experience, and love they bring into our lives.

Lord, we pray that you continue to bestow strength upon our seniors, enabling them to fight the good fight, run the race, and keep the faith, as mentioned in 2 Timothy 4:7. May they find renewed vigor in their journey and serve as inspiring examples to generations behind them.

We ask, Lord, that you make our seniors acutely aware of your great and everlasting love for them. In Psalm 103:17, your Word assures us that "the steadfast love of the Lord is from everlasting to everlasting on those who fear him." May they feel your loving presence surrounding them, comforting them in moments of solitude.

We pray earnestly, Lord, that you fill our seniors with the abundant grace of your Holy Spirit. Just as the Holy Spirit descended upon the disciples in Acts 2, may your Spirit empower and guide them daily. Grant them wisdom, discernment, and understanding as they navigate the seasons of life.

And for those among our seniors who have not yet come to know you personally, Lord, we pray that your gentle call may resonate within their hearts. Your invitation is open, and your arms are wide. May they hear your loving voice saying, *"Come, my son, come, my daughter, I am waiting."* (Revelation 3:20).

In addition to these prayers, Lord, we lift up the specific needs and concerns of our seniors. We pray for their physical health, emotional well-being, and financial security. Surround them with caring individuals who can offer support and companionship.

We also pray for our senior citizens' homes and assisted living facilities, that they may be places of comfort, respect, and safety. Bless the caregivers and staff who serve our seniors with compassion and kindness.

Heavenly Father, we thank you for the invaluable presence of our seniors in our lives. May they continue to shine as beacons of your love and wisdom, and may we always honor and cherish the golden legacy they represent. In the name of Jesus, we pray. Amen.

Personal Prayer Guide

Use this page for your personal prayers and impressions. You can use this to write the names of people you are praying for and record testimonies of what God is doing through prayer.

CHAPTER 12

PRAYER FOR THE CHURCH AND GOD'S WORK

Evil in front of the church

In the year 2020, our church witnessed a remarkable transformation right before our eyes. A family had moved into a modest two-room house directly across from our church building. Little did we know that this humble abode would soon evolve into a bustling hub and a center of communal activity.

I felt a strong conviction to introduce myself to our new neighbors, to engage in conversation with them, and to extend an invitation to our church services. At first glance, it seemed as though they were already familiar with matters of faith and Christianity. Nevertheless, I persisted in my efforts, refusing to give up on the potential for spiritual growth and connection.

On one occasion, I had a conversation with one of the family members who shared a poignant request, saying, "Please pray for me, for I once served the Lord, but now I have strayed." This plea deeply resonated with me, and I yearned to learn more about their spiritual journey, though initiating a meaningful dia-logue proved to be challenging.

As time went on, I began to uncover a startling truth about our new neighbors—they were reputed individuals with a notorious criminal history within our city. They had become, in a sense, the untouchables of our community. What's more, their interactions with local law enforcement, including drinking and smoking together, raised serious concerns.

Within the church, we were subjected to incessant phone calls em-anating from the vicinity, offering substantial sums of money, job opportunities, and lucrative business propositions, among other enticements. This continued unabated for many months, causing immense frustration and distress among our congregation.

I resolved to extend an invitation to these individuals, particularly the homeowner, to embrace the love of Christ. However, my at-tempts were met with evasiveness on his part. Yet, amidst these challenges, a remarkable development unfolded—the Lord's divine touch reached the hearts of the young men residing in that house. They made a profound decision to accept Jesus as their Lord and Savior, and I had the privilege of baptizing them.

Yet, the prevailing injustice and moral decay occurring right outside our church doors continued unabated. Despite the prox-imity of a police officer stationed nearby, no action was taken to address the situation.

In response, I called upon our congregation to engage in a three-day period of fasting and fervent prayer. On the culmination of our fast, I stood before our church's transparent wooden doors, raising my hands in supplication. I beseeched the Lord, saying, "Today, Lord, I implore you to lead these individuals to renounce their way of life and follow You. May they experience a transformation in Your light, or may they be led to leave this place."

In the ensuing weeks, a glimmer of hope emerged as the wife of the household began attending our church services. Eventually, they decided to relocate from their residence to another location.

Dear friends, this testimony serves as a testament to the power of prayer and the faithfulness of our Lord. Your prayers possess a might that exceeds any worldly force. Your prayers can dismantle the strongest fortresses and move mountains. It is a reminder that through fervent prayer, the unimaginable can transpire.

Let us never underestimate the potency of our prayers. As a church, let us continue to believe in the transformative power of our Lord and His work among us.

The Bible says, *"little children (believers, dear ones), you are of God, and you belong to Him and have [already] overcome them [the agents of the antichrist]; because He who is in you is greater than he (Satan) who is in the world [of sinful mankind] "*– 1 John 4:4 (AMP).

PRAYER FOR THE POLICE

Heavenly Father, today we come before you with hearts full of gratitude for the dedicated men and women who serve in law enforcement and for their families who share in their sacrifices. Your Word in Numbers 6:24-26 inspires us to pray: *"The Lord bless you and keep you; the Lord make his face shine on you and be gracious to you; the Lord turn his face toward you and give you peace."*

Lord, we earnestly pray for our police officers and their families. May your divine protection surround them like a mighty shield, guarding them from harm, both in their daily duties and personal lives. Let your peace reign within their homes, and may your presence be a constant source of strength and comfort.

Father, we humbly beseech you to keep their hearts pure and their actions just. Protect them from the temptation to misuse their authority or position and instill in them a sense of integrity and compassion that mirrors your own.

We lift up the daily movements of our law enforcement officers, Lord. Be their guiding light in the midst of darkness, their refuge in times of trouble, and their source of wisdom in moments of uncertainty. Let them feel your protective hand over their lives.

We pray for the breaking of any chains of addiction, trauma, or stress that may have taken hold in their lives. In accordance with 1 Peter 5:7, we cast all their anxieties on you, knowing that you care for them deeply. May they experience your loving embrace and find healing from the wounds of their profession.

Lord, remind our police officers that their lives are precious to you, as declared in Psalm 139:14: "I praise you because I am fearfully and wonderfully made." May this truth resonate in their hearts and give them hope.

For those among them who do not yet know Jesus as their Lord and Savior, we pray for their salvation. Open their hearts to receive your grace, and may they come to know the transformative power of your love. We also lift up those officers who may be facing personal struggles, such as divorce or other challenges; we ask for your divine intervention and comfort in their lives.

In closing, we thank you, Lord, for the service and sacrifice of our police officers and their families. May your blessings continue to flow upon them, and may they find strength, guidance, and salvation through faith in your Son, Jesus Christ. In His name, we pray. Amen

PRAYER FOR THE BODY OF CHRIST

"May He grant you out of the riches of His glory, to be strengthened and spiritually energized with power through His Spirit in your inner self, [indwelling your innermost being and personality], so that Christ may dwell in your hearts through your faith. And may you, having been [deeply] rooted and [securely] grounded in love, be fully capable of comprehending with all the saints (God's people) the width and length and height and depth of His love [fully experiencing that amazing, endless love]; and [that you may come] to know [practically, through personal experience] the love of Christ which far surpasses [mere] knowledge [without experience], that you may be filled up [throughout your being] to all the fullness of God [so that you may have the richest experience of God's presence in your lives, completely filled and flooded with God Himself". Ephesians 3: 16-19

Heavenly Father, on this glorious morning, we gather as one body, the Body of Christ, representing every corner of the globe. With hearts united, we bring before you your beloved sons and daughters from every tongue, nation, tribe, and family. We are reminded of your promise in Philippians 4:7, which says, *"And the peace of God, which transcends all understanding, will guard your hearts and your minds in Christ Jesus."*

Lord, we earnestly pray that you pour out your blessings upon each and every one of us. May your divine peace, which surpasses all human understanding, be a constant presence in our lives. As we navigate the challenges of this world, may your peace guard our minds, anchoring us in the love of Christ.

Today, we lift our voices in prayer, asking that your love flows through us to the farthest reaches of the earth. Let us shine brightly as beacons of your love, hope, and grace, illuminating the lives of our friends, families, and nations. May our actions and words reflect the light of Christ dwelling within us.

Grant us, O Lord, the strength to stand unwavering in our commitment to honor you and resist the temptations of the enemy. In the face of adversity, may we remain steadfast in our faith, knowing that you are our refuge and fortress.

For those among us who are enduring hardships, facing persecution, battling depression, or feeling the weight of burnout and sickness, we humbly ask for your healing touch. Stretch forth your hand, O Lord, and bring restoration, comfort, and renewed strength to their lives. Let your abundant mercies fall upon them like the gentle rain of a new morning.

Lord, use each one of us as laborers for the great harvest, as vessels of your grace and messengers of your truth. We long to see your kingdom expand, and we thank you for the privilege of being your instruments in this world.

In closing, we give you all the glory and praise, O Lord. Thank you for the unity and fellowship we share as the Body of Christ. May your blessings continue to flow abundantly upon us, and may we shine brightly for your name's sake. We pray all of this in the precious name of our Savior, Jesus Christ. Amen.

Our Church

Heavenly Father, we humbly bow before you in prayer, lifting up your beloved church, scattered across the nations, to your loving care. Your Word in Matthew 16:18 reminds us that "the gates of hell shall not prevail against [your church]." We thank you for the assurance of your presence and protection.

Lord, we earnestly pray for your bride, the church, to continue in the diligent preparation of her oil, as described in Matthew 25:4, that her lamp may burn brightly until the glorious return of our Savior. Strengthen her resolve to seek you fervently in prayer, worship, and study of your Word.

We implore you, Father, to grant your body discernment and wisdom to discern and combat the lies and accusations that seek to sow division and discord among her members. May your church stand firm, rooted in truth and love.

In a world where sin is rampant, we pray for your saints to pursue holiness and sanctify themselves, as instructed in 1 Thessalonians 4:3. May they be beacons of righteousness, even in the face of prevailing darkness.

Father God, we ask for your intervention against the spirits of immorality and division that threaten the unity of your church. In the name of Jesus, we rebuke these forces and pray for unity and harmony within your body.

Turning our hearts to the church in Congo, we lift her up in prayer. We pray for stability, revival, and a return to her first love and mission. Pour out your anointing upon her, Lord, that she may shine brightly as a witness for your glory.

Come, Lord Jesus, and reign over your church. We beseech you to ignite the flames of prayer and praise within her once more, as described in Acts 2. Release the gifts of the Holy Spirit upon every believer, that they may prophesy, dream dreams, and see visions according to Acts 2:17.

We pray for the raising up of leaders within your church—prophets, apostles, evangelists, pastors, and teachers—to equip and edify the body of Christ, as Ephesians 4:11 instructs.

In the powerful name of Jesus, we cast out the spirits of coldness, conformity, competition, and comparison from your church. Replace them with the spirit of sonship, as Romans 8:15 reminds us that we cry, *"Abba, Father."*

Lord, our hearts hunger and thirst for you. Satisfy our souls with your presence and your Word. May your love abound more and more within your church, and let your light shine brightly in her heart, as we are reminded in Philippians 1:9.

We thank you for your abiding presence among us. Awaken us, Lord, to hear and obey your voice without hesitation. Break the spirit of confusion that clouds our minds and lead us into your perfect will.

Come, Lord Jesus, and have your way in your church. May she rise up in strength, unity, and purpose to proclaim your glorious name to the ends of the earth. In your precious name, we pray. Amen.

Personal Prayer Guide

A LETTER TO
THE CONGOLESE CHURCH

Dear Church in Congo,

It is estimated by the Pew Research Center that the number of Christians from various denominations in the Congo exceeds 63 million, comprising roughly 95.7 percent of the national population or about 2.9 percent of the global Christian community.

Have you noticed this astonishing statistic? Nearly 95.7 percent of the population is believed to be Christian in our nation. Churches, are you aware of this fact?

In our streets, a church can be found on every corner, and preachers are a common sight on every street. On Saturdays, prayer sessions are held almost everywhere. Yet, each morning we awaken to news describing the horrors that transpired the night before.

Every day, we witness church divisions that lead to clashes among members and pastors. This year, social media has been flooded with reports of revered and prominent men of God falling short, succumbing to immorality. Conflicts among church leaders have become all too frequent.

Politicians can scarcely speak without quoting scripture. Dear churches, when we examine the state of politics, traffic on our roads, and the activities within our churches today, we must ask ourselves, has a malevolent force infiltrated our congregations, remaining undetected?

Dear churches, what has become of our love for our neighbors? Where is the emphasis on valuing others above ourselves?

Dear churches, what has happened to our prayer life?

Dear fellow church members, has the clamor of weapons drowned out the power of our prayers?

Dear Churches,

What has become of you? Are your words drowning out your actions?

Dear Church, do you require an evangelist?

Dear Church, what has befallen you? Are you still the salt of the earth, or has your essence been diluted? What will become of you?

Dear Church, where is your light? Who will illuminate this world if your radiance is already dimmed by it?

Dear Congolese Church,

I implore you to venture out to your roundabouts and streets. Observe the traffic, then return to your sanctuaries and scrutinize the turmoil within your congregation. This tumult stretches from leadership to the ordinary members. Reflect on how you clamor to be at the forefront, even when lagging behind others.

Dear Congolese Church, I urge you to visit the chambers of parliament in our nation.

Then, revisit your churches and witness the dissonance between your words from the pulpit and your deeds after stepping down. Contemplate the discord among your politicians, mirroring the strife within your congregations. Notice how these political leaders exploit the people for their self-serving gains, only to discard them once their purpose is fulfilled. Acknowledge the corruption that festers among them and recognize the same corruption within your own ranks.

Dear Congolese Churches, who will reveal the truth to the world and set it on the right path? If you remain divided among yourselves, who will effect change in this nation while relying on those who steal, offer you luxury cars, and buy you houses?

Dear Church, draw near to God with a contrite heart, and He will draw near to you. Purify your hearts, you double-minded, and cleanse your hands, you sinners.

Dear Church, I address you to awaken from the spell of materialism, the allure of fame, the addiction to position, the paralysis of power, and the enticement of wealth and immorality.

Awaken, Church, from spiritual numbness, for you are teetering on the brink of a great fall.

Rise up and don the servant's attire.

Rise up and wear the prophet's mantle; prophesy to the nation.

Rise up, become spiritual shepherds after God's own heart, and nourish the people with knowledge and true understanding.

Dear Church, much has been entrusted to you, and much will be required of you.

Dear Church, I implore you to build your foundation on the rock.

Dear Church, open your eyes and perceive the looming precipice.

Dear Church, reflect on your ways and return to the Lord.

Dear Church, repent on behalf of yourselves and your people.

Dear Church, it's time to step out. You were never meant to hide under the table but to shine on the mountaintop for all to see.

Dear Church, Christ has never been divided, so cease dividing His people.

Dear Church, listen to Me, says the Lord, and you shall be saved.

Dear Congolese Church, heed the voice of the Lord and revive.

Dear Congolese Church, if you are reading this, know that the Lord desires to restore you as a lampstand to shine once more.

Now, decide how you will respond to this call.

Dear Congolese Church, behold, I stand at the door and knock. If you hear My voice and open the door, I will come in and dine with you.

BIOGRAPHY

Roland and his wife Ingeborg serve as pastors at 'Eglises Christ Glorifié' (Glorified Christ Church), a thriving multisite congregation deeply committed to preparing the bride to meet her bridegroom, Jesus Christ, and spreading His message to the two million people in the city of Goma, in eastern Congo. 'Eglises Christ Glorifié' is characterized by its vibrant prayer life, powerful worship, and impactful preaching of the Word. This church embraces a diverse congregation of all ages.

For three years, Roland worked diligently with refugees in Uganda, equipping them with self-reliance business skills and language literacy. Additionally, he collaborated with Justice Rising in efforts to support child soldiers.

Roland is the founder of ACTION URUMA, a growing organization dedicated to providing thousands of children and young men with equal access to free education and healthcare. The organization focuses on education, maternal and child health care and discipleship.

Roland holds a master's degree in leadership and church growth, as well as a degree in Human Resources management. He also completed a program at the Harvest School of Mission in Mozambique.

Roland's unwavering passion is to share the message of Christ wherever he goes. He is committed to witnessing families, communities, and nations come to the saving knowledge of Jesus Christ."

Personal Prayer Guide

Use this page for your personal prayers and impressions. You can use this to write the names of people you are praying for and record testimonies of what God is doing through prayer.

Personal Prayer Guide

Printed in the USA
CPSIA information can be obtained
at www.ICGtesting.com
LVHW071133270424
778639LV00012B/96